THE PRIDE

COLLECTED EDITION

THE PRIDE VOL. 1: I NEED A HERO Contains material originally published in magazine form as THE PRIDE #1-6 and THE PRIDE ADVENTURES #1-3 and the CARDIFF INDEPENDENT COMIC EXPO ANTHOLOGY. First printing 2016. Self-published by Joe Glass under the banner of Queer Comix. © 2011 Joseph Glass and Gavin Mitchell. The Pride, its logo, all prominent characters featured therein and all other character likenesses therein are trademarks of Joseph Glass and Gavin Mitchell, unless otherwise noted. Queer Comix logo is trademark of Joseph Glass and Mike Stock. All rights reserved. No part of this publication may be reproduced or transmitted in any form or by any means (except for review purposes) without the express written permission of the authors. All names, characters, events & locales in this publication are entirely fictional. Any resemblance to actual persons (living or deceased), events without satiric intent, is coincidental unless otherwise stated. Printed in the UK by UK Comics. 1st Printing. The Pride and The Pride Adventures logos designed by Jason Gann. Wraparound cover by Ricardo Bessa

ThePrideComic.co.uk | Facebook.com/ThePrideComic | @ThePrideComic | ThePride.bigcartel.com

CONTENTS

FOREWORD

Being a superhero is hard... Being a gay superhero is harder. In a world that's overrun with people of special abilities and things that are "different" what does it mean to actually be "different?" The Pride is a team of individuals who unlike their-at least seemingly-hetero counterparts, accept everyone they come in contact with... unless of course that person is a megalomaniacal Reverend with designs on world domination. Though honestly, with a little rehabilitation I'm sure he could sit with us too. *The Pride* is one of those books that parallels real-life struggles with the weighty decisions anyone in spandex has to make: to kill or not to kill, that is the question. It's about deciding what kind of hero you want to be. It's about accepting how you were born and convincing the world to accept you too.

Often times we take for granted the struggles of others. I'll admit, I've had a relatively easy time being as gay as I am. *The Pride* reminded me of a more entertaining *Queer as Folk* in that yeah the drama is heightened and personal struggles are punctuated with explosions but they still parallel people in our own world. It reminded me to check my vodka soaked drag-queen induced privilege and keep mindful that everyone's path is different. There are those out there who may seem "better off" but it took quite a fight to get there. *The Pride* isn't about the obvious insinuation of proudness or the connotation of a parade with free condom and lube samples, but more about coming together and accepting your common man, woman, non-binary person, and radioactive sewer mutant with an understanding that we all have a fight to win. Whether that's just to have our pronouns recognized, to overcome stereotypes, or just live on the surface with the rest of society...

Like everyone, each of the characters has their own personal struggle with acceptance, but they manage to find that common thread that bonds them together: peace. There's something we could all learn from the adventures of The Pride, it's that no matter who or what you are, you can always find your pride.

-DAX!

RUNNING ORDER

HOLDING OUT FOR A HERO

Written by Joe Glass, Art by Gavin Mitchell, Colors by Kris Carter, Letters by Mike Stock

FIREWORKS

Written by Joe Glass, Art by Gavin Mitchell, Colors by Kris Carter, Letters by Mike Stock

DON'T RAIN ON MY PARADE

Written by Joe Glass, Art by Dan Harris, Colors by Kris Carter, Letters by Mike Stock

YOU THINK YOU'RE A MAN

Written by Joe Glass, Art by Gavin Mitchell, Colors by Kris Carter, Letters by Mike Stock

CABARET

Written by Joe Glass, Art by Kendall Goode (pages 105-112), JD Faith (pages 113-115), Gavin Mitchell (pages 116-117), Jack Davies (pages 118-119), Chris Wildgoose (pages 120-123) & Marc Ellerby (pages 124-126), colors by Ben Wilsonham (pages 105-115 & pages 124-126), Letters by Mike Stock

FINALLY

Written by Joe Glass, Pencils by Maxime Garbarini, Inks and Colors by Héctor Barros, Letters by Mike Stock

The Pride Issue 1 - Cover by Kris Anka

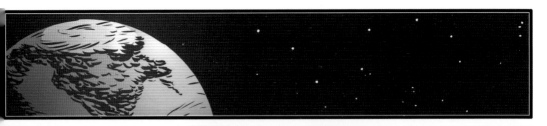

WRITTEN BY JOE GLASS

ART BY GAVIN MITCHELL

HOLDING OUT FOR A HERO!

THAT'S IT, DORK! NO MORE EVIL EDUCATION STREAMS FROM YOU, MAN!

I'M GONNA KICK YOUR BUTT!

YOU SHALL NEVER DEFEAT ME, SUPER-MORON!

I'LL HELP YOU, FRIEND!

A FAGMAN FIGURE?

WHY THE PERVO FIGURE. YOU LIKE QUEERS, BILLY, HUH? HA HA.

HA HA!

SHUT UP... SHUT UP...

YEAH, FAGMAN, HA!

HA HA. IS THAT YOUR FAVE HERO? DO YOU LUUURVE FAGMAN?

SHUDDUP, SHUDDUP SHUDDUP!!

FABMAN IS GREAT! FABMAN IS...

COLOURS BY KRIS CARTER

LETTERS BY MIKE STOCK

11

12

LONDON

≷GROAN≷

NOW, NOW, DEAR. DON'T MOAN.

IF ONE DOES NOT WISH TO BE TAUGHT A LESSON IN HOW TO TREAT A LADY...

...ONE SHOULD NOT APPROACH *THE MASTER*.

HONEY, I FIGURE THESE GUYS HAVE LEARNED THEIR LESSON WELL.

AH, IF IT ISN'T OUR *FABULOUS* YANKEE DARLING. WHAT BRINGS YOU TO THIS *DELIGHTFUL* LITTLE CORNER OF THE WORLD?

I'VE A PROPOSITION TO MAKE, FROST.

DARLING, I HAD *NO IDEA* YOU SWUNG BOTH WAYS.

EW. NO. I'M THINKING OF SETTING SOMETHING *UP.* I'M CALLING A MEETING OF SOME OF THE *BEST* GUYS AND GIRLS I KNOW, OVER IN NEW YORK.

MMHMM, DARLING. AND WHY SHOULD I COME ALONG TO THIS LITTLE GET-TOGETHER OF YOURS? I'M A BUSY WOMAN. LOTS OF *NAUGHTY* BOYS AND GIRLS OUT THERE.

I FIGURED YOU'D *LOVE* THE CHANCE TO TEACH THE WORLD A LESSON.

THE HEAD-MISTRESS HERSELF HELPING TO SET THE RECORD STRAIGHT.

WELL, IT *HAS* BEEN A WHILE SINCE I GRACED THE COLONIES WITH MY PRESENCE. THE *USUAL PLACE,* I TAKE IT?

SURE, WHY CHANGE WHAT WORKS.

OF COURSE. WELL, IT *IS* AN INTERESTING PROPOSITION. DO SEE THAT YOU DON'T BORE ME.

los angeles

WHAT UP, AMIGOS! HOW 'BOUT YA DROP TH' ROCK, AND LET *UNCL'* TYRONE MAKE YOUS A DEAL, EH?

UMM?

WE JUST PLAYIN' BALL, DUDE. WE DON'T WANT NO TROUBLE.

AIN'T *NO TROUBLE* YOU CAN BRING I AIN'T READY FOR, JUNIOR...

Y'SURE 'BOUT THAT, TY?

WHITE TRASH... *CHICA*, WHAT YOU DOIN' HERE? I AIN'T *PLAYIN'* NO GAME.

NAH, CUZ. BUT THESE KIDS *WERE.* THEY DON'T NEED ANY OF YOUR TROUBLE. *OR* ANY OF WHAT YOU'RE SELLING.

SORRY, *'CUZ'*, BUT NO ONE STEPS ON TYRONE, 'SPECIALLY NO FAGGOTY, @$$-LOVIN' SONOVA--

BLAM BLAM BLAM

BAD MOVE, TY.

FIVE MINUTES LATER...

THANKS, WT!

DON'T MENTION IT. JUST DO ME A FAVOUR...

... *DON'T* GET MIXED UP WITH TY'S CROWD. 'THE LIFE' AIN'T *NO LIFE* AT ALL.

SURE THING, WT!

AND HEY, WE KNEW YOU AIN'T *NO FAG.* YOU *KICKED ASS!*

I'D HAVE HELPED, BUT YOU SEEMED TO HAVE IT UNDER CONTROL. BUT THAT ASSUMPTION THEY HAD ABOUT US 'FAGS'... IT RUINS THE GOOD FEELING EVERY TIME, HUH?

FABMAN. PLEASURE TO MEET YOU.

I KNOW WHO YOU ARE. PLEASURE'S ALL MINE, MAN.

BUT THEY WERE JUST KIDS, DUDE. ATTITUDES CHANGE.

NOT QUICK ENOUGH THOUGH, RIGHT?

I'M LOOKING TO DO SOMETHIN' ABOUT THAT. YOU WANT IN?

...SURE.

new york city

HEY, *FRUITIE!* WHATCHA RUNNIN' FO'?

OOOF!

CRASH

HEY, I THOUGHT YOU *QUEERS* WAS MEANT TO BE GRACEFUL.

HEH, MEBBE HE'S JUST TOO *EXCITED* TO SEE US.

BIG BURLY MEN LIKE *US.* SISSY-BOY *MUST* BE TURNED ON.

P-PLEASE, J-JUST LEAVE ME ALONE, I'M NOT DOING ANYONE ANY HARM.

THAT'S WHERE WE FEEL DIFFERENTLY, *SICKO.* AIN'T *NO* PLACE FOR YOU *HERE,* OR *ANYWHERE.*

YEAH. THIS IS JUST A *PUBLIC SERVICE* 'BOUT TO HAPPEN HERE.

SIN! SIN AND CORRUPTION!

MURDERERS!!

SEE HOW YOU LIKE IT, *MURDERER!*

FEAR NOT, SISTER. *NO HARM* SHALL COME TO YOU THIS DAY.

AS FOR YOUR ASSAILANT... FOR HIM I MAKE *NO* SUCH PROMISE.

EEP!

SMAK

YOU ARE THE ONE THEY CALL FABMAN. WELL MET!

RIGHT BACK AT YA! QUEEN SAPPHIRE, RIGHT?

INDEED. THOUGH THE PEOPLE OF THIS COUNTRY HAVE COME TO KNOW ME AS *'MUSCLE MARY'*.

IT IS AN AMUSING MONIKER.

IT REMINDS ME OF THE *GOOD* YOUR PEOPLE HAVE TO OFFER.

SOMETHING THIS GUY IS BY FAR THE OPPOSITE OF.

IF YOU'D LIKE TO SEE SOME *MORE* GOOD, AND MAYBE *DO* SOME GOOD ALONG THE WAY... I HAVE AN OFFER FOR YOU.

19

FINE, FINE. *THE S.L.G.B.T.*

WE'RE GETTING OFF TRACK. THE REASON I CALLED YOU ALL HERE...

WELL, AREN'T YOU *FED UP* OF BEING MIS-REPRESENTED OUT THERE?

OF BEING A LAUGHING STOCK BECAUSE YOU OPENLY DISPLAY YOUR LIFESTYLE *AS WELL AS* YOUR SUPER-POWERS?

OR SICK THAT THE ONLY GAY PEOPLE YOU SEE ON TV ARE THESE *DESEXUALISED*, NON-THREATENING *JOKE MACHINES.*

HELL, THERE'S THE *AWESOME HERO ARRANGEMENT* (AHA!), THE *WONDROUS WARRIORS*, THE *TRULY GREAT SIX*, THE *FAMOUS FIFTY*, EVEN THE SUPER HEROIC ORGANISATION OF *EAST CORNWALL!*

BUT WHERE IS THE *GAY* SUPER GROUP? WHERE ARE THE *TRANSGENDER* HEROES?

WELL, YOU KNOW WHAT? THEY AIN'T OUT THERE. SO, THAT'S WHY I PROPOSE WE START *OUR OWN!*

HOW 'BOUT IT? WILL YOU ALL JOIN *THE PRIDE?*

UMMM, EXCUSE ME?

I'M HERE FOR THE S.L.G.B. MEETING--

21

S.L.G.B.T.!!

SHHH!

AND YOU ARE?

UMMM, MY NAME IS OWEN MERCURY. I, UMMM, DON'T HAVE A SUPER NAME. YET.

I JUST... I KEPT MY EAR TO THE GROUND. HEARD THIS MAY BE GOING ON, AND... WELL, I'D LIKE TO JOIN.

I CAME ALL THE WAY UP FROM SAN FRAN. I'M GAY. I WANT IN.

WELL, OKAY THEN OWEN. WHAT IS IT YOU CAN DO?

OH! HOLD ON...

HE DOES KNOW THIS ISN'T AN AUDITION FOR PORNOGRAPHY, YES?

QUIET, GIRL! LET THE BOY DO HIS THING.

UH, HONEY, WHAT ARE YOU DOING?

SLAM!

LONG TIME NO SEE, WOLF.

FABS. WELCOME TO THE PARTY.

PULL UP A STOOL.

OOOH, YOU KNOW HOW I *LOVE* PARTIES. WHERE'S THE GO-GO BOY?

AT TOYBOI. NOT EXACTLY ONE OF THOSE BARS, DUDE, SO TONE IT DOWN A NOTCH, WOULD'YA.

⇒SIGH⇐ FINE. YOU *KNOW* HOW MUCH I HATE HIDING MY FABULOUSNESS, DARLING.

IT'S EASY FOR YOU, WHAT WITH ALL YOUR PRACTICE IN THE CLOS--

DID YOU JUST CALL ME 'DUDE'?

THINGS CHANGE, QUEENY. THERE, HAVE A DRINK.

⇒HACK⇐ ⇒COUGH⇐ ~HUR~ ⇒ECH⇐!

BUT THEN SOME THINGS NEVER CHANGE.

HI, OH, HI. OOH, DON'T YOU LOOK THE *BAD* BOY!

YES. UMM, I'D LIKE A COSMO, PLEASE.

YOU KNOW WHAT? WHISKEY IS FINE.

WHAT DO YOU WANT?

THAT'S NICE.

FINE. I HAVE A PROPOSITION FOR YOU.

HOW MANY TIMES DO I HAVE TO SAY 'NO'?

HAHAHA, YOU'RE SO FUNNY I FORGOT YOU WERE SAD.

I'M PUTTING TOGETHER A TEAM, DEAR. I WANT YOU IN IT.

DON'T DO TEAMS. DON'T HERO NO MORE.

FUNNY. A LOT OF THE CRIMINAL ELEMENT SEEMS TO BE GETTING CAUGHT AROUND HERE LATELY. *VIOLENTLY,* I MIGHT ADD.

YOU ALWAYS WERE A BAD BOY, DEAR.

27

WOLF! OH MY GOD, I'M --I'M *SUCH* A BIG FAN OF YOUR WORK!

UMM, THANKS, KID. AND YOU ARE?

THAT'S TWINK. NEW RECRUIT. ISN'T HE THE SWEETEST?

ERM, YEAH. I JOINED THE PRIDE, I'M JUST HOPING TO DO SOME GOOD Y'KNOW.

I'M LOOKIN' FORWARD T--

ULP!

CHRIST, FABS, ARE YOU *NOT* BOTHERING TO TRAIN THEM?

TO BE HONEST, I TRAINED MYSELF. NOT AS RIGOROUS AS YOU, BUT I TRIED TO FOLLOW YOUR METHODS, I-

WE ONLY STARTED *YESTERDAY*, WOLFIE. I WAS HOPING YOU'D HELP WITH THAT.

HERE, KID.

YA DID GOOD. NOTHING A LITTLE TRAINING WON'T IMPROVE.

SO YOU'RE IN?

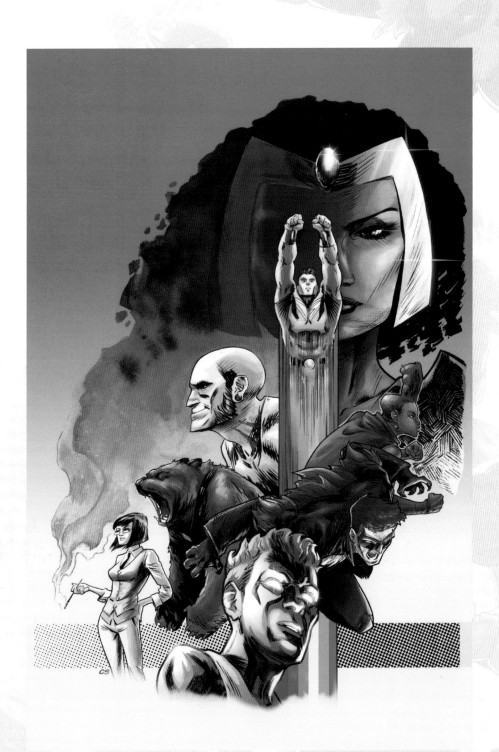

The Pride Issue 2 - Cover by Cory Smith and Kris Carter

fireworks

JOe Glass
WRITER

GAVIN MITCHELL
ART

KRIS CARTER
COLOURS

MIKE STOCK
LETTERS

THAT WAS AWESOME TO SEE, MR... ERM, WOLF, SIR

NAMES BRIAN, KID. AND THANKS.

ODD OF YOU TO GIVE UP THE LEADERSHIP ROLE LIKE THAT, STEVE.

PLEASE. I MAKE A GREAT FRONT MAN FOR THE MEDIA, BUT YOU HAVE THE EXPERIENCE AND THE TRAINING.

I WANT TO IMPROVE THE WORLD'S PERCEPTION OF US. THAT'S NOT GONNA HAPPEN WITH A POORLY TRAINED TEAM. AND YOU'RE REALLY GOOD AT THE GRUNT WORK ANYWAY, DARLING

WELL, THAT WAS ALMOST A COMPLIMENT, FABS.

I SAY IT WITH LOVE, BRIAN. TOODLES. YOU BOYS PLAY NICE, NOW.

HERE, KID.

TH-THANKS.

WHOOPS.

AND IT'S OWEN, OWEN M—

MERCURY, YEAH I KNOW. I CHECKED YOU OUT ON OUR WAY OVER HERE.

OH.

DON'T WORRY, OWEN. I DO IT TO EVERYONE. IT'S A DETECTIVE THING. I LIKE TO KNOW EVERYTHING THAT'S GOING ON IN A ROOM.

OH. RIGHT. I GUESS. AFTER ALL, I KNOW A LOT ABOUT YOU, YOU BEING IN JUSTICE DIVISION AN' ALL. I NEVER UNDERSTOOD WHY YOU LEFT THOUGH.

I DIDN'T 'LEAVE'. I WAS FIRED.

OH.

UMM, WHY? IF THAT'S OKAY TO ASK?

HN.

YEAH. IT'S ONLY FAIR, KID.

THEY CALLED A MEETING. THEY DIDN'T SAY WHAT IT WAS FOR.

DUDE, AWESOME! TAKE A SEAT.

I'LL STAND THANKS. WHAT'S THIS ABOUT?

ME AND THE GUYS JUST HAVE SOME, LIKE, CONCERNS DUDE, AND WE THINK, LIKE, MAYBE IT'D BE WISE IF YOU COULD STEP DOWN.

WHAT?!

LOOK, IF YOU'RE CONCERNED ABOUT ME AND FABS, WE'RE NOT REALLY DATING OR ANYTHING. THAT'S ALL WILD SPEC—

DUDE, DUDE, CHILL.

IT'S NOT ABOUT WHETHER YOU GUYS ARE REALLY AN ITEM.

I DON'T—

IT'S ABOUT WHETHER YOU'RE PERCEIVED TO BE.

IT'S THE IMAGE IT CREATES.

WOLF, MY FRIEND, IT IS AS SIMPLE MATTER AS THIS: WE NEVER ASKED IF YOU ARE IN FACT GAY, BUT PEOPLE BELIEVE YOU ARE. IF YOU AREN'T THEN PERHAPS WE CAN COME UP WITH ANOTHER SOLUTION.

ARE YOU GAY?

... YES.

THEN THERE'S THE ISSUE, DUDE. WE HAVE A FAMILY-FRIENDLY IMAGE WE HAVE TO PROTECT, OR PEOPLE WON'T THINK ABOUT US THE SAME WAY ANYMORE.

THEY WON'T FEEL SAFE.

I'M SORRY, MAN, BUT I'M SURE YOU UNDERSTAND.

IT'D JUST, LIKE, LOOK BETTER IF YOU LEAVE THAN WE FIRE YOU, Y'KNOW?

AND THAT WAS THAT. THE END OF MY CAREER WITH THE DIVISION. AND BEING OUTED ALL IN ONE.

OH MY GOD, THOSE GUYS ARE JERKS! THERE MUST BE SOMETHING WE CAN DO?

NAH, IN A WAY THEY WERE RIGHT. THEY PROBABLY WOULD HAVE STARTED GETTING DAMAGING PRESS FROM SOME CORNERS OF THE MEDIA.

WHICH IS WHY FABS' PLAN MAY BE A GOOD ONE AFTER ALL. IMPROVE HOW PEOPLE SEE US.

EVEN IF IT IS THE FIR' PLAN THAT HE EVER STUCK '

BESIDES, I GET THE FEELING THEY WEREN'T ALL TOTALLY FOR THE IDEA. VENUSIAN ACTUALLY LOOKED KIND O' ASHAMED.

YOU THINK HE'S GAY?

NO, NO. HIS SPECIES HAVE NO CONCEPT OF GENDER.

TO EVEN CALL HIM MALE IS WRONG. IT'S JUST A FORM HE CHOOSES SO PEOPLE WOULD UNDERSTAND HIM.

HUH...YOU'RE PRETTY GOOD AT READING PEOPLE THEN, HUH?

GOTTA BE, KID.

SO YOU AND FABMAN NEVER—

OH GOD, NO!

HE'S JUST A FRIEND. HA!

COOL.

COOL?

OH, WOW, LOOKIT THE TIME!

GOTTA GET UP EARLY, GET READY FOR PRACTICE TOMORROW, LONG DAY, WHOO BOY, WHERE DOES THE TIME GO, HUH! OMG, NIGHT!

ERR, NIGHT?

SO WHAT'S THE WORD, BOSS.

THE WORD IS GOOD, AND TH' NAME IS REVEREND, BASHER. YOU'D DO WELL TO 'MEMBER THAT.

BUT THESE RESULTS. THE SCIENTISTS WERE RIGHT... BEFORE THEY ALL DIED, ANYWAY. THE PROCESS AIN'T QUITE WORKIN' YET.

AH NEED SOMETHING MORE. ANOTHA ELEMENT TO TH' PROBLEM I AIN'T QUITE GOT YET.

TH' DAMN X-CEL VIRUS, THE SUPERHUMAN SICKNESS IN MANY OF THE SO-CALLED 'HEROES' OF THIS DECADENT, SINFUL WORLD; THE IMMUNOLOGY IS SO STRONG IT ACT'LLY FIGHTS AGAINST MAH COMMANDS.

AH NEED A SPECIAL KIND O' SUPER. AH AIN'T FOUND IT YET...

...BUT BELIEVE ME, AH'M GONNA KEEP LOOKIN'.

39

YOU EVER GONNA CHANGE THAT DAMN TRUCK, HARV?

HEY, SHE STILL RUNS AND PURRS LIKE A KITTEN. WHY CHANGE WHAT WORKS?

HONEY, THIS THING AIN'T NEVER WORKED.

I LIKE WHAT I KNOW, ANGEL.

WELL, THIS TEAM THING IS NEW TO US, DARLIN'. WHAT YOU MAKIN' OF IT?

I DUNNO. COULD WORK. COULD BE A MASSIVE DISASTER.

BUT HEY, FABS MEANS WELL, AND IT'S WORTH A SHOT.

YOU KNOW ME, ALWAYS TRYIN' TO MAKE A GOOD IMPRESSION.

FIERCE, HONEY.

FIERCE.

YOU SURE YOU'RE UP TO THIS, HARVEY?

I'M FINE, ANGEL.

40

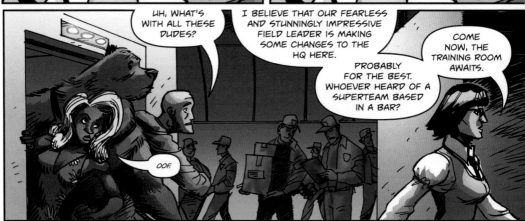

BRRRAAAAAAH!

CLANG!

YOU FOUGHT WELL, YOUNG WARRIOR.

YEAH, YOU DID GOOD, KID.

THANKS.

HOWEVER, THAT GUARD WASN'T PERFECT. THERE WERE AT LEAST FIFTEEN POSSIBLE TAKE-DOWN POSITIONS AVAILABLE TO THE QUEEN HERE, AT LEAST TWO OF WHICH WERE POTENTIALLY LETHAL.

YOU MAY BE ARMOURED UP, KID, BUT WE HAVE NO IDEA OF THE LIMITS OF THAT ARMOUR YET.

ENOUGH!

YOUR FIGHTING TECHNIQUE WAS OF COURSE FLAWLESS, YOUR MAJESTY.

PLEASE, YOU MAY CALL ME BY MY BIRTH NAME, SAPPHIRE, BRAVE WOLF.

THANK YOU. IT IS AN HONOUR.

IF I MAY SAY THEN, YOU DIDN'T SEEM TO GIVE MUCH REGARD TO MY POSITION BEHIND YOU. YOU'VE FOUGHT ALONE FOR SO LONG, YOU'VE BECOME USED TO IT. NOW YOU FIGHT WITH A TEAM AGAIN, YOU MAY WANT TO BE MORE AWARE OF THOSE THAT FIGHT WITH YOU.

moments later

I CAN'T GO IN.

WHAT?

MY METAL ARMOUR WOULD JUST HEAT UP IN THERE. I'D BE A DANGER TO ANYONE INSIDE.

HN. GOOD CALL.

HEAD AROUND BACK. IF THERE'S ANYONE TRYING TO GET OUT THAT WAY, YOU CAN HELP THEM.

ANGEL!

YOUR POWERS TO CREATE CONFUSION COULD BE A PROBLEM TOO. YOU STAY OUT HERE ON CROWD CONTROL.

SURE THING, HONEY!

YOU HEARD THE MAN, DARLINGS! NO ONE'S GETTING PAST THIS LINE.

WHAT LIN– ⇒OOF⇐

THAT ONE, HONEY!

BEAR? CAN'T GET ANY SCENTS. OVER THE SMOKE AND MY OWN BURNING FUR, ANYWAY.

I CAN'T SEE ANYTHING EITHER. WE NEED TO CLEAR SOME OF THESE FIRES!

FROST!

ALREADY DONE, DARLING. I'M GETTING THIS PLACE UNDER CONTROL.

KREAAAA!

SISTER!

FROST, ARE YOU WELL?

I'M FINE, DEAR. MY, BUT YOU ARE A STRONG ONE.

AYE, AS ARE YOU TO SHOW NO FEAR IN THE FACE OF SUCH DISASTER. A WARRIOR BORN, PERHAPS?

SIMPLY BRITISH STIFF UPPER-LIP, MY DEAR.

WELL, THE FIRE'S DEAD HERE NOW. CAN YOU PICK UP ANYTHING?

THUDD

ACK. WHAT THE
ELL HAPPENED
ERE ANYWAY,
OLF?

I DON'T KNOW. I COULDN'T SEE ANY EVIDENCE OF ACCIDENTAL FIRE OR EXPLOSION OUT FRONT, BUT THERE WASN'T ANY ACCELERANT EITHER. IT'S LIKE THE PLACE SPONTANEOUSLY COMBUSTED.

THAT'S RIDICULOUS.

EXACTLY.

DON'T YOU SCUM COME NO CLOSER, OR THESE FAGGOTS GET TO BURN HERE AS WELL AS TH' FIRES O' HELL!

FIREBOMB!

WELL, THAT MAKES SENSE.

M CLEANSING
HIS DEN OF SIN! LET
Y RIGHTEOUS FIRE
URN THIS WORLD OF
ODOMITES AND
ERVERTS ONE BAR AT A
ME! NOW I'LL GET TO
AKE OUT TWO OF THE
OST FAMOUS OF THE
VERTS WITH THESE
INNERS!

ONE STEP AT A TIME, I'LL CLEAN THIS WORLD FOR THE MASTER RACE TO RISE ONCE MORE.

STARTING HERE!

NO!

HUH?

The Pride Issue 3 - Cover by Cory Smith and Kris Carter

I, UH, I'M JUST GOING TO GET SOME AIR.

OWEN? YOU OKAY, KID?

UH, SURE, I... I, UMMM, I---

YOU DIDN'T KNOW I WAS HIV POSITIVE.

NO, I--

TNK!

UH, SORRY. NERVES.

IT'S OKAY.

I GUESS, I JUST HAVEN'T EVER MET ANYONE WHO WAS POSITIVE BEFORE--

THAT YOU KNOW OF.

YEAH, AND WELL, I GUESS I DON'T KNOW MUCH ABOUT IT AND WELL, ISN'T IT...

ISN'T IT KIND OF DANGEROUS? I MEAN, GIVEN WHAT WE DO...

YOU MEAN, CAN YOU CATCH IT?

NO!

...YES...

I'M SO SORRY.

KID, YOU HAVE NOTHING TO APOLOGISE FOR. NO ONE EVER TALKS ABOUT THIS, AND FEW EDUCATE ABOUT IT. HELL, IT WAS NEVER MENTIONED TO ME GROWING UP.

TO ANSWER YOU'RE CONCERNS, NO, YOU CAN'T JUST CATCH IT.

AIN'T NOTHIN' WE'RE GONNA DO THAT PUTS YOU AT RISK. IT PASSES THROUGH BODILY FLUIDS, NOT BODY CONTACT. AND I'M HOPIN' YOU'RE NOT PLANNIN' ON A LOT OF THAT HAPPENING.

HEH, NO.

BUT, I MEAN, IS IT HEALTHY FOR YOU? AREN'T YOU, TECHNICALLY, LIKE, ILL?

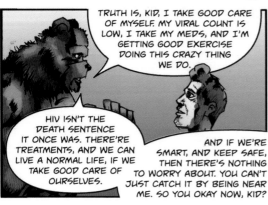

TRUTH IS, KID, I TAKE GOOD CARE OF MYSELF. MY VIRAL COUNT IS LOW, I TAKE MY MEDS, AND I'M GETTING GOOD EXERCISE DOING THIS CRAZY THING WE DO.

HIV ISN'T THE DEATH SENTENCE IT ONCE WAS. THERE'RE TREATMENTS, AND WE CAN LIVE A NORMAL LIFE, IF WE TAKE GOOD CARE OF OURSELVES.

AND IF WE'RE SMART, AND KEEP SAFE, THEN THERE'S NOTHING TO WORRY ABOUT. YOU CAN'T JUST CATCH IT BY BEING NEAR ME. SO YOU OKAY NOW, KID?

YEAH...THANKS, YEAH, THAT HELPED. SORRY FOR GETTING ALL WIGGED OUT BY IT.

NOT AT ALL, KID. SADLY, IT HAPPENS ALL THE TIME.

HEY GUYS!

WE ARE GETTING, LIKE, LOADS OF CALLS FROM THE MEDIA RIGHT NOW, AND I COULD REALLY USE THE HELP.

ALL HANDS ON DECK!

SO, OKAY GUYS, MAYBE WE SHOULD CALL IT A DAY WITH THIS.

I THINK WE MAY NEED TO GET SOMEONE IN HERE FULL TIME TO DO THIS KINDA THING. I COULD USE SOME HELP WITH THAT WOLF.

SURE.

BUT DON'T WORRY, I WON'T BE ASKING YOU GUYS TO DO THIS AGAIN.

GOOD, BECAUSE THIS WAS A COLOSSAL WASTE OF OUR TIME.

IF WE'RE GOING TO BE A SUPERHERO TEAM OUT THERE IN THE THICK OF IT, WE'VE GOT TO TRAIN.

I UNDERSTAND WHAT YOU'RE TRYING TO DO, FABS, BUT ACTIONS SPEAK LOUDER THAN WORDS. WE SHOULD MAKE SURE OUR ACTIONS COUNT.

TWINK... YOU LOOK LIKE YOU'VE SEEN A GHOST.

OH. HA, NO NOT A GHOST. ON THE PHONE... IT WAS MY MOM AND DAD...

I'VE... I'VE NOT SPOKEN TO THEM IN A WHILE. NOT SINCE THEY SENT ME TO SOME CAMP; TO "CURE" ME OF MY POWERS.

IT'S A LONG STORY.

WELL, KID, YOU KNOW WHERE I AM. YOU NEED TO TALK, I'M HERE.

...THANKS. THAT MEANS A LOT.

63

antabulosa

STEPHEN? ARE YOU OKAY?

YES. NO. ARE YOU?

I MEAN, THAT WHOLE DRAMA EARLIER... WHAT A MESS.

WERE THEY RIGHT? ARE WE DOING THE RIGHT THING? DID THIS WORLD REALLY NEED AN LGBT SUPERHERO TEAM?

WHY NOT? IT'S A DIVERSE WORLD, BUT SOMETIMES, WHEN WE LOOK AT THE HEROES OF THIS PLACE... CAN YOU SEE THAT?

LOOK AT THE JUSTICE DIVISION?

OUT OF A TEAM AS BIG AS THEY ARE, ONLY ONE MEMBER IS BLACK.

ONLY TWO ARE WOMEN, AND THEIR NEVER THE SPOKESPERSONS FOR THE TEAM. AND MORNINGSTAR TOO IS RARELY SEEN AS A FACE FOR THE TEAM.

THEY'RE SO WORRIED OF OFFENDING THE SENSIBILITIES OF A BIG, WHITE WORLD, THEY'RE TOO SCARED TO CELEBRATE THEIR DIFFERENCES.

THIS TEAM... AS WELL AS RIGHTING WRONGS AND FIGHTING FOR JUSTICE, WE CELEBRATE WHAT'S DIFFERENT.

WE CAN SHOW PEOPLE WE'RE UNAFRAID, AND THAT'S AN IMPORTANT MESSAGE TO GET OUT THERE. FOR EVERYONE.

YOU'RE RIGHT.

I JUST HOPE WE'RE READY.

TO BE CONTINUED...

The Pride Issue 4 - Cover by Jack Lawrence

SOMEONE'S GOT MY SON!
YOU THINK YOU'RE A MAN
WRITTEN BY JOE GLASS
ART BY HÉCTOR BARROS
COLOURS BY NATHAN ASHWORTH
LETTERS BY MIKE STOCK

OH MY GOD, *JAKE*!

YOU HAVE A SON?

BEFORE MY POWERS KICKED IN, BEFORE I CAME OUT... I WAS MARRIED. *TO A WOMAN*.

WHEN I FIGURED OUT WHO I WAS... SARAH LEFT ME. AND SHE WAS *PREGNANT*.

WE WERE ESTRANGED FOR YEARS, BUT SHE NEVER KEPT JACOB A SECRET FROM ME. HE'S THE THING I'M *PROUDEST* OF IN THIS WORLD...

...AND NOW SOME MONSTER CALLED *BASHER* HAS HIM!

WE'LL SAVE YOUR SON, BEAR, BUT WE SHOULD WAIT UNTIL MORNING. FIND OUT WHAT WE CAN ABOUT THIS *BASHER* CHARACTER.

BUT--!

WE DON'T WANT TO GET *BEATEN* AGAIN, LIKE WE DID WITH JUSTICE DIVISION TODAY.

WE'LL, *ALL* OF US, WE'LL SORT THROUGH THIS THING. BUT YOU *NEED* TO COOL OFF.

WHAT?

RRRRAAA-AARRRGH!

YOU CAN 'COOL OFF'! I'M FINDING MY SON!

SMASH

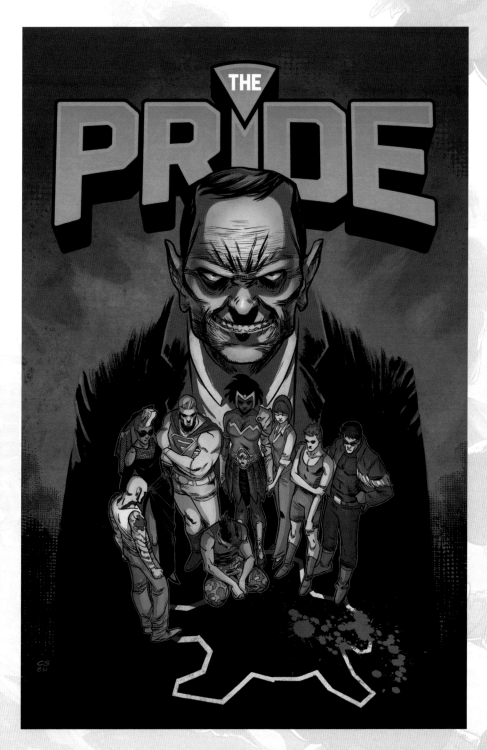

The Pride Issue 5 - Cover by Cory Smith and Ben Wilsonham

YOUR FATHER WAS A *GOOD MAN*, JAKE. HE'LL *ALWAYS* BE WITH US.

BASHER CAN *NEVER* TAKE THAT AWAY FROM YOU.

THANKS, TWINK.

DUDE, YOU CAN CALL ME OWEN.

BUT I'M STILL GONNA FIND BASHER.

AN' I'M GONNA MAKE HIM PAY.

KID, REVENGE IS *NEVER* THE WAY.

THAT BEING SAID, YOU CAN JOIN US, *AT LEAST* 'TIL WE FIND YOUR FATHER.

BUT... I'M *NOT* GAY, WOLF. I'M NOT LIKE MY DAD THAT WAY.

DOESN'T MATTER. THAT'S *NOT* WHAT WE'RE ABOUT.

TH-THANK YOU.

IT'S OKAY, KID. YOU GOT US.

HEY, IT'S OK, IT'S—

UH, *WHO'S THAT?*

WE'RE GONNA *GET* THE MUTHA WHO DID THIS TO HIM, JAKE. YOU CAN *BET YOUR ASS* WE WILL.

I HEAR YA.

≥SIGH≤ LOOK AT ME ≥SNF≤

STILL, *GREAT* TURN OUT FOR THE MAN.

THOUGH WHERE'RE FABS AND W.T.?

FABS HAS TAKEN IT *REALLY* HARD. WAYNE WENT LOOKING FOR HIM.

UH-HUH... WELL, I NOTICE *FROST* AIN'T HERE EITHER.

ALWAYS KNEW SHE WAS A *COLD* ASS B--

I SEE YOU ARE TAKING THE LOSS OF OUR FALLEN COMRADE-IN-ARMS WELL.

COME NOW, DEAR, MEN DIE ALL THE TIME.

NO SENSE IN ALL THAT FUSS AND DRAMA.

I THINK PERHAPS YOU FEEL MORE THAN YOU LET ON, SISTER.

PIFFLE. HE WAS A FINE FELLOW, AND NOW HE'S GONE. YET HERE WE ARE, SO WE MAY AS WELL CARRY ON WITH OUR LIVES.

HA! NOT EVEN YOU ARE SO COLD A BEAST!

HE WAS A FINE MAN, TRUE. AND A WARRIOR. HE WAS ONE OF US.

THERE'S NO SHAME IN LETTING YOURSELF FEEL IT, YOU KNOW.

YOU DON'T HAVE TO BE AFRAID.

AFRAID! HOW DARE--

HE... WAS A *GOOD* MAN...

AYE. HE WAS. JUST THE EXAMPLE I WAS LOOKING FOR. MY PEOPLE WOULD HAVE RESPECTED HIM.

HE SHOULDN'T HAVE DIED.

I SHOULD HAVE BEEN BETTER... I SHOULD'VE...

QUIET. YOU DID EVERYTHING YOU COULD. YOU WERE AMAZING.

I HAVE SEEN YOU IN BATTLE, I *KNOW* THE WARRIOR THAT YOU ARE.

I-

SAPPHIRE... I NEED TO TELL YOU-

HUSH, EVANGELINE...

I KNOW ALL I NEED TO KNOW...

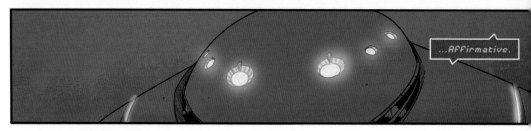

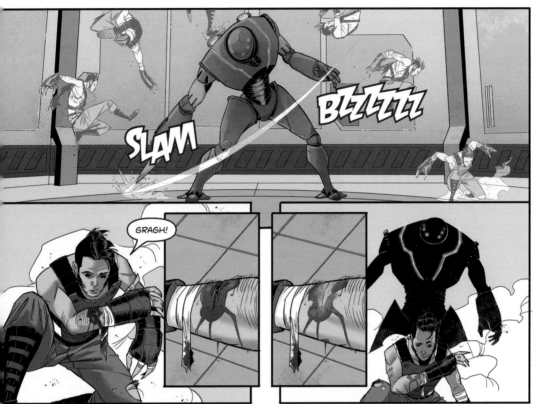

A FEW HOURS LATER

BWUH! FERRETS!

WUH-WOLF?

BRIAN? ARE YOU DOWN HERE?

THE LAB!

I KNOW WHERE THEY ARE.

UH, GUYS, YOU NEED TO COME UP HERE.

NOW!

TO BE CONTINUE

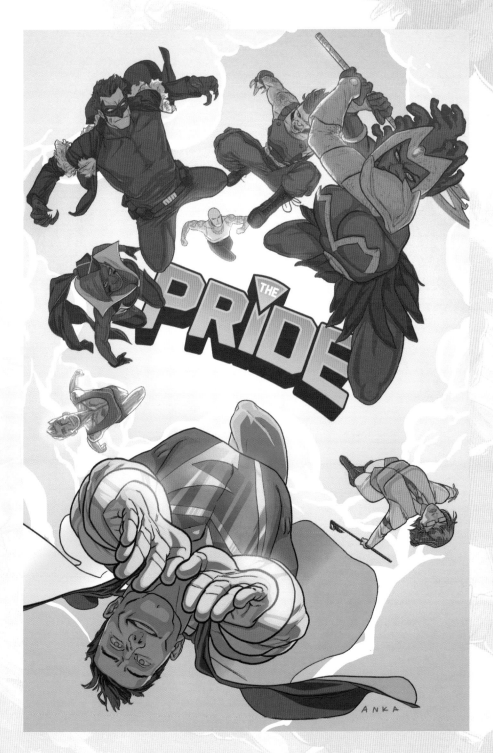

The Pride Issue 6 - Cover by Kris Anka

128

129

HOW DID YOU FIGURE OUT WHERE THEY ARE?

THE SAND AT THE SCENE OF BEAR'S... BEATING.

IT WAS *DIFFERENT*, FINER THAN THE CONSTRUCTION SAND AT THE SITE, AND *MILDLY* RADIOACTIVE, ACTUALLY.

SO?

SO, IT MATCHES RECORDED SAMPLES OF SAND FOUND IN AN AREA OF THE NEW MEXICO DESERT, WHERE ATOMIC TESTS WERE CARRIED OUT *DECADES AGO.*

WHOA, WHOA, WHOA NOW, HONEY. RADIATION? ATOMIC?

THE RADIOACTIVITY HAS CREPT DOWN TO SAFE LEVELS NOW, JUST *SLIGHTLY* MORE THAN STANDARD BACKGROUND RADIATION.

BUT IT'S NOT THE *RADIATION* THAT WORRIES ME.

THIS GUY DOES.

HIS NAME IS REVEREND FRANKLIN PHILLIPS. HE IS AN *ACTUAL* ORDAINED MINISTER, BUT HE WAS EXCOMMUNICATED *YEARS AGO.*

HE'S A SICK MAN THAT USES RELIGION AS A WEAPON, THAT'S FOR SURE.

TWINK'S BASICALLY RIGHT. AND LIKE MOST MEN OF THAT ILK, HE'S *A HYPOCRITE.* SEE, PHILLIPS IS X-CEL POSITIVE TOO.

HE HAS A POWER TO CONVINCE PEOPLE OF THINGS BY SPEAKING TO THEM. HE WAS THROWN OUT OF THE CHURCH FOR USING IT ON HIS PARISHIONERS.

BEFORE, HIS POWERS NEVER SEEMED ABLE TO WORK ON OTHER X-CEL POSITIVE PEOPLE. THIS MACHINE OF HIS SEEMS TO HAVE CHANGED THAT, AND BROUGHT HIS INFLUENCE *GLOBAL.*

HE'LL HAVE AN ARMY. WE'RE SOME OF THE FEW PEOPLE UNAFFECTED. THIS IS GOING TO BE *HARD.* WE NEED TO BRING OUT OUR A-GAME, PEOPLE.

OH, HONEY, IT IS *BROUGHT!*

YOU SEE WHAT HE'S DONE TO MY DAD?

AIN'T *NO WAY* HE'S GETTIN' AWAY WITH THAT.

GOOD. THE CRUISER IS THE FASTEST JET ON THE PLANET. WE'RE NEARLY THERE.

GET READY.

139

142

DAD!

FROST, CAN YOU FREEZE *JUST* THE NON-ORGANIC ELEMENTS OF THE MACHINE? *WITHOUT* HURTING BEAR?

I CAN TRY.

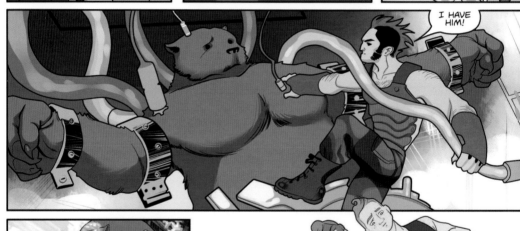

I HAVE HIM!

NOW, TWINK!

GGRRAAADSSH

OH, DAD... I'M SO SORRY... I'M SO SORRY...

...WHA... F'R...?

146

YOU DID IT, THEN. YOU SAVED THE WORLD.

SURE DID, KIDDO. 'D I COULDN'T 'AVE DONE IT 'THOUT YOUR 'NSPIRATION.

HERE. I GOT THIS TO THANK YOU, BILLY.

OH MY GOD, THANK YOU, FABMAN!

I WANT YOU TO HAVE THIS.

Y'KNOW, TO REMIND YOU.

BILLY, I COULDN'T...

IT'LL REMIND 'OU THAT YOU ME A LONG WAY, ? YOU FOUGHT A HARD FIGHT, AND... WELL, AND...

AND NOW EVERYONE SEES YOU AS THE HERO YOU ARE. JUST LIKE I ALWAYS DID.

THANK YOU, BILLY.

153

written by **JOE GLASS**   pencils by **MAXIME GARBARIN**

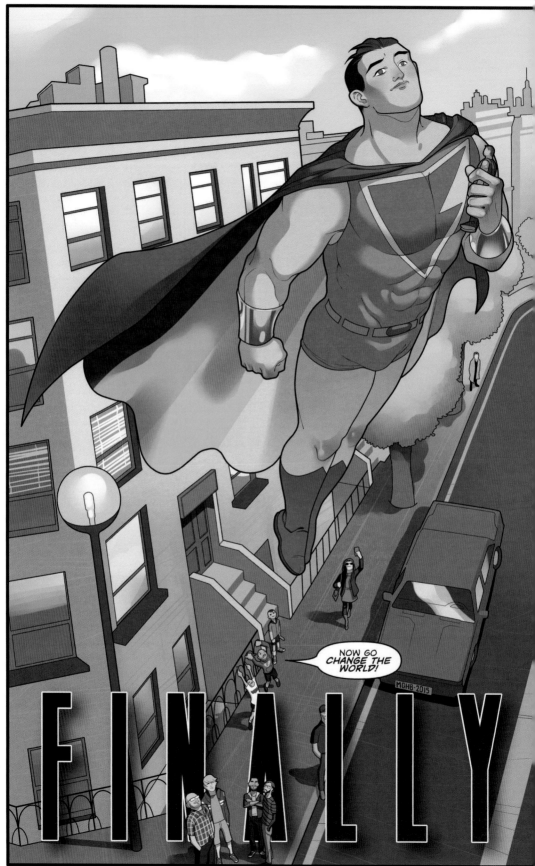

inks & colours by **HECTOR BARROS**   letters by **MIKE STOC**

155

RUNNING ORDER

IT GETS BETTER

Written by Joe Glass, Art and Letters by Gavin Mitchell, Colors by Kris Carter

RIDE THE PAIN

Written by Joe Glass, Art by Samir Barrett, Letters by Mike Stock

IN THIS SHIRT

Story by Joe Glass, Lyrics by Jaime McDermott and The Irrepressibles, Art by Joshua Faith, Colors by Kris Carter, Letters by Mike Stock

THE PRIDE VS. THE PRIDE

Written by Joe Glass, Art by Chris Wildgoose, Colors by Ben Wilsonham, Letters by Mike Stock

MOVING FORWARD

Written by Joe Glass, Art by Denis Medri, Colors by Ben Wilsonham, Letters by Mike Stock

LADIES NIGHT

Written by Joe Glass, Art by Dani Abram, Letters by Mike Stock

A DETECTIVE CALLS

Written by Joe Glass, Art by Joshua Faith, Colors by Ben Wilsonham, Letters by Mike Stock

OUTRAGE

Written by Joe Glass, Layouts by Cory Smith and JD Faith, Art by JD Faith, Colors by Ben Wilsonham, Letters by Mike Stock

YOU CAN'T GO HOME AGAIN

Written by Joe Glass, Art by Martin Kirby, Colors by Ben Wilsonham, Letters by Mike Stock

THE MORNING AFTER

Written by Joe Glass, Art by Adam Graphite, Letters by Mike Stock

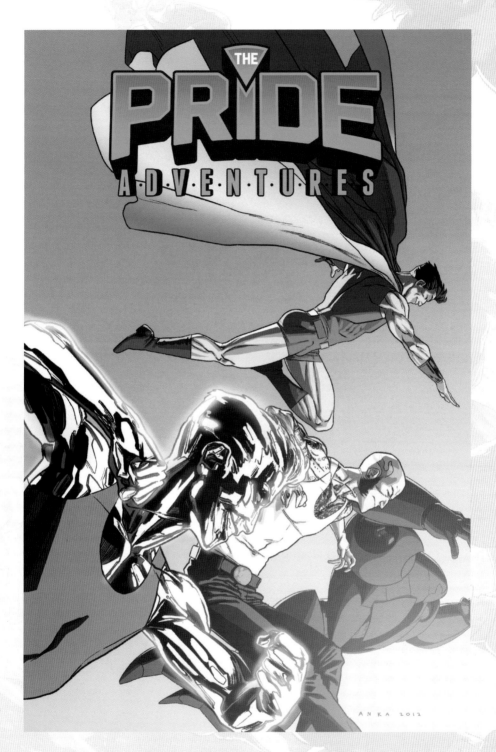

The Pride Adventures Issue 6 - Cover by Kris Anka

158

NOT YOU! THERE COULDN'T POSSIBLY BE A WORSE A PERSON TO COME AND 'SAVE' ME!

>SIGH< I GET THAT A LOT.

LOOK, KID, WHATEVER IT IS, I'M SURE IT'S NOT THAT BAD...

NOT THAT BAD? THEY KNOW! DAMMIT, THEY CAUGHT ME WITH HIM, AND THEY'RE GOING TO TELL EVERYONE AND... AND... THEY KNOW I'M GAY!

THEY'RE GOING TO RUIN ME. MY LIFE... MY LIFE IS OVER...

OH.

OH HONEY, I'M SO SORRY. BUT THIS ISN'T THE WAY TO SOLVE THIS. IT'S REALLY NOT BELIEVE ME...

DON'T! I KNOW WHAT YOU'RE GOING TO SAY, THAT I HAVE SO MUCH TO LIVE FOR, AND THAT I SHOULD FACE THIS ALL HEAD ON, BUT IT'S CRAP!

MY LIFE IS RUINED. MY FRIENDS... MY FRIENDS WILL HATE ME, MY FAMILY... THEY... THEY WON'T LOVE ME ANYMORE... YOU DON'T KNOW ANYTHING!

I'VE SEEN YOU ON THE NEWS, SO PROUD AND FLYING YOUR FLAG... WELL, IT MUSTA BEEN SO EASY FOR YOU, BUT THAT'S NOT ME, DUDE!

YOU'RE RIGHT. I AM GOING TO TELL YOU ALL THOSE THINGS, AND THEY'RE TRUE, SWEETIE, TRUST ME...

AND MAYBE I WON'T KNOW EXACTLY HOW THINGS WILL HAPPEN OR WHEN, BUT I KNOW THEY'LL IMPROVE...

BUT YOU'RE WRONG ABOUT ONE THING. IT WASN'T ALWAYS EASY FOR ME... AND I DO KNOW WHERE YOU ARE RIGHT NOW.

BECAUSE I WAS HERE MYSELF WHEN I WAS NOT MUCH YOUNGER THAN YOU.

160

I ALWAYS KNEW THAT I WAS DIFFERENT, BUT THAT DOESN'T MEAN IT WAS ALWAYS EASY FOR ME.

THE WORST PART WAS EVERYONE ELSE KNEW I WAS DIFFERENT TOO...

...AND THE GUYS ON THE FOOTBALL TEAM PUT TWO AND TWO TOGETHER AND FOR THE FIRST TIME IN THEIR LIVES GOT IT RIGHT.

THAT MADE IT WORSE IN A WAY. IT FELT LIKE I HAD A DIRTY LITTLE SECRET AND EVERYONE KNEW IT, AND I WAS ALMOST DESERVING ALL THIS.

I STILL HADN'T COME TO LOVE AND RESPECT MYSELF, AND SO I DIDN'T HAVE THE STRENGTH TO STAND UP FOR MYSELF.

FAGGOT

COULDN'T SEE HOW ANYONE'S LIFE COULD BE ANY WORSE THAN MINE. AND THAT'S WHEN I THOUGHT 'WHY BOTHER?'

AND SO I CAME HERE...

WHY DID YOU CHANGE YOUR MIND?

OH, HONEY, I JUST DECIDED THAT I WAS BETTER THAN WHATEVER THEY THREW MY WAY.

AND WHO CARES IF THEY KNEW ABOUT ME... I LIKED WHO I WAS, AND I GOT MORE COMFORTABLE WITH IT EVERY DAY.

NOW LOOK AT ME!

WHAT'S YOUR NAME, SWEETIE?

TOMMY. TOMMY CLEMENTS.

I'VE NEVER TOLD ANYONE ABOUT THAT NIGHT, TOMMY. NOT EVEN MY PARENTS KNOW. BUT NOW YOU DO.

WHY TELL ME?

BECAUSE I CARE, TOMMY. AND YOU OBVIOUSLY CARED ABOUT ME ENOUGH TO STICK AROUND AND LISTEN TO ME TOO.

HERE. THESE ARE THE NUMBERS YOU CAN CALL WHEN YOU NE SOMEONE TO TALK TO, AND PLACES TO GO IF YOU NEED HELP.

BECAUSE THERE ARE PEOPLE WHO CARE ABOUT YOU, TOMMY. LOTS OF THEM.

AND I DON'T KNOW HOW THINGS WILL GO. THE WORLD CAN BE HARD, AND EVERYTHING MAY SEEM BAD AT FIRST. BUT PEOPLE DO CARE ABOUT YOU, AND I PROMISE YOU IT GETS BETTER.

IF YOU WANT TO JUMP STILL... I WON'T STOP YOU.

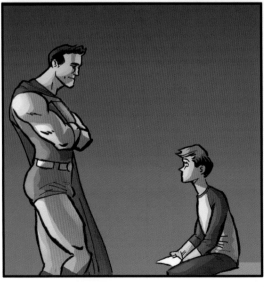

...THANK YOU.

THANK YOU, TOMMY. THANK YOU.

AND IN TEXAS TODAY, BILLY CARDONI WAS FOUND DEAD AFTER HAVING TAKEN A LETHAL DOSE OF PRESCRIPTION PAINKILLERS IN A SADLY SUCCESSFUL SUICIDE ATTEMPT. THE BOY REPORTEDLY COMMITTED SUICIDE OVER ALLEGED HOMOPHOBIC BULLYING AT HIS SCHOOL IN AUSTIN, TEXAS. BILLY'S PARENTS ARE 'INCONSOLABLE' AT THE LOSS OF THEIR SON, DESCRIBED BY FRIENDS AND FAMILY AS 'EXUBERANT, HAPPY AND FULL OF LIFE'.

TEEN GAY SUICIDE

HE WAS JUST THIRTEEN YEARS OF AGE.

OH GOD...

Fantab

ABRAHAM LINCOLN HIGH SCHOOL

BROOKLYN, NEW YORK

OH GOD, TOMMY! I'M SO GLAD YOU'RE OKAY!

TOM, DUDE, NO ONE CARES, REALLY. THOSE TOOLS WENT WAY TOO FAR.

IT'S OKAY. I GOT YOU GUYS. IT'LL BE TOUGH SOMETIMES...

YEAH, MAN. BUT, DUDE, WE'RE YOUR FRIENDS... AND YOU'RE THE SAME GUY YOU ALWAYS WERE.

IF ANYONE GIVES YOU ANY TROUBLE...

T IT GETS ER, DUDE.

IF YOU EVER FEEL LIKE YOU NEED TO TALK TO SOMEONE; LIKE THE WORLD IS TOO TOUGH AND YOU JUST WANT SOMEONE TO LISTEN TO YOU FOR A CHANGE.

THANK YOU.

PLEASE DON'T HESITATE TO CONTACT ONE OF THESE WONDERFUL ORGANISATIONS. THE GOOD MEN AND WOMEN THERE CARE ABOUT YOU, AND WANT TO HEAR FROM YOU.

IN THE US: CONTACT THE TREVOR PROJECT ON 866-4-U-TREVOR (866-488-7386)

IN THE UK: CONTACT CHILDLINE ON 0800 11 11 OR GO TO www.childline.org.uk OR www.stonewall.org.uk

AND HEAR MESSAGES FROM ACROSS THE WORLD AT: www.itgetsbetter.org

SEE, BUT NOW I'M CONFUSED AGAIN.

THAT PUNCH WOULD HAVE LEVELLED MOST GUYS.

YOU DON'T HAVE A SCRATCH OR BRUISE ON YOU. YOU'RE POWER MAKES YOU INVULNERABLE.

SO HOW HAVE YOU EVEN GOT ALL THOSE TATTOOS WHEN *NO* NEEDLE SHOULD BE ABLE TO BREAK YOUR SKIN?

COME WITH ME, KID, I'LL SHOW YOU HOW IT'S DONE.

WHEN I WAS LITTLE, MY DADDY WOULD HIT ME.

THIS ONE TIME, HE HIT ME *SO DAMN HARD* THAT I WENT DOWN THE STAIRS AND BROKE MY ARM.

THAT WAS WHEN HE'D HEARD THAT I'D BEEN SEEN KISSING A BOY FROM DOWN THE STREET.

I'M SORRY, W.T., I HAD *NO IDEA...*

HE TOLD ME, 'AIN'T NO *GOOD FAGGOT* BUT A *DEAD FAGGOT*, SO DON'T *MAKE ME* WISH YOU WAS DEAD, BOY'.

TO THIS DAY, HE DON'T SPEAK TO ME AND I DON'T SPEAK TO HIM.

THE POWERS WORK BASED ON MY CONFIDENCE.

BUT IT'S *HARD* TO BE CONFIDENT WHEN YOU'VE GOT ALL THOSE *HORRIBLE DAYS* IN THE DARK PARTS O'YOUR HEAD.

SO EVERY NOW AND THEN, WHEN I FEEL THE NEED, I GO GET SOME NEW INK.

AND I RUN INTO ALL THOSE DARK CORNERS IN MY SKULL, AND I LET IT WASH OVER ME.

AND AS THAT NEEDLE BREAKS MY SKIN, I RIDE THE PAIN. I RIDE IT AS FAR AWAY AS IT'LL GO.

AND I THINK THAT'S THE LAST THOSE TIMES WILL EVER HURT ME AGAIN.

Y'KNOW, YOU HAVE GOT TO BE TOUGHEST GUY I HAVE *EVER* MET.

HA! SAYS TH' DUDE WITH THE *METAL ARMOUR SKIN*.

YEAH, WELL, MY ARMOUR IS *JUST* METAL, DUDE...

...YOURS IS *ALL YOU*.

I AM LOST.

IN OUR RAINBOW, NOW OUR RAINBOW...

...IS GONE.

OVERCAST, BY YOUR SHADOW.

AS OUR WORLD'S MOVE ON.

IN THIS SHIRT

I CAN BE YOU...TO BE NEAR YOU...FOR A WHILE...

IN THIS SHIRT, I CAN BE YOU, TO BE NEAR YOU.

FOR A WHILE.

THERE'S A CRANE, KNOCKING DOWN

ALL THESE THINGS

THAT WE WERE.

I AWAKE

IN THE NIGHT

TO HEAR THE ENGINES PURR.

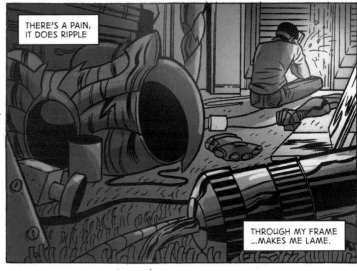

THERE'S A PAIN, IT DOES RIPPLE

THROUGH MY FRAME ...MAKES ME LAME.

THERE'S A THORN, IN MY SIDE

IT'S THE SHAPE, IT'S THE PRIDE

OF YOU AND ME, EVER CHANGING, MOVING ON NOW...MOVING FAST

AND HIS TOUCH, MUST BE WANTING

MUST BECOME FREE TO ACT

BUT I NEED

NEED TO TELL YOU, THAT I LOVE YOU, IT NEVER RESTS

I AM LOST.

LEWIS MARTELL

OUTRAGE

A HERO TO MANY

IN THIS SHIRT

Story by JOE GLASS, lyrics by JAMIE
MCDERMOTT and THE IRREPRESSIBLE

Art by JOSHUA FAITH, colours by
KRIS CARTER, letters by MIKE STOCK

The Pride Adventures Issue 2 - Cover by W Scott Forbes

THE **ONGOING** SPATE OF BANK ROBBERIES IN THE CITY CONTINUED THIS MORNING, AS THE **GRIFFIN BANK** FOUND ITSELF THE **LATEST** TARGET.

THE THIEVES **ESCAPED** THE SCENE WITH **FIVE MILLION DOLLARS** IN CASH, LEAVING **FOUR** PEOPLE WOUNDED. ONE MAN IS IN **CRITICAL** CONDITION.

THE GROUP RESPONSIBLE FOR THE CRIMES, WHO HAVE SO FAR **EVADED CAPTURE** BY THE AUTHORITIES, **APPEAR** TO BE SETTING THEMSELVES UP AS A NEW **SUPERVILLAIN TEAM**, AND HAVE INDICATED THAT THEY **WILL** BE STRIKING AGAIN, POSSIBLY AS SOON AS THIS AFTERNOON.

CALLING THEMSELVES—

THE **PRIDE!**

YOU **COWER** BEFORE US LIKE **MEWLING, BABY ZEBRAS**. WE ARE THE **TOP** OF THE FOOD CHAIN, AND **YOU** ARE **OUR PREY.**

WE WILL SOON TAKE **OUR RIGHTFUL** PLACES AS **RULERS** OF THIS CITY. ALL WILL BOW BENEATH US, IN **AWE** OF OUR **MAJESTY!**

HONEY, I DON'T KNOW WHAT'S **WORSE**...

THE PRIDE VS. THE PRIDE

WRITTEN BY PJ MONTGOMERY
ART BY CHRIS WILDGOOSE
COLOURS BY BEN WILSONHAM
LETTERS BY MIKE STOCK

END.

SAN FRANCISCO IS THE **LEADING** FINANCIAL AND CULTURAL CENTRE FOR THE NORTHERN CALIFORNIAN AREA.

IT HAS SEEN **MANY** INCREDIBLE THINGS, FROM THE **PROGRESSION OF HUMAN RIGHTS**, MEN AND WOMEN **STANDING TALL** TO SPREAD MESSAGES OF **PEACE** AND **TOGETHERNESS**...

IT HAS ALSO SEEN **TERRIBLE** AND **DEVASTATING** THINGS.

ISLANDS WHERE THE **CONDEMNED** WERE **SHIPPED AWAY, OBLITERATING** NATURAL DISASTERS...

AND **NOW**, AN **INVASION FORCE** UNLIKE **ANY** IT HAS SEEN BEFORE.

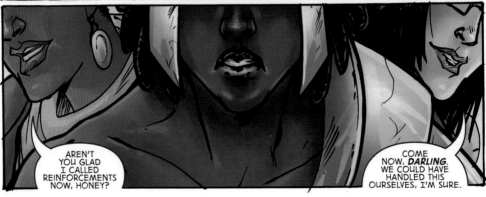

AREN'T YOU GLAD I CALLED REINFORCEMENTS NOW, HONEY?

COME NOW, **DARLING**. WE COULD HAVE HANDLED THIS OURSELVES, I'M SURE.

MOVING FORWARD

WRITTEN BY *JOE GLASS* ART BY *DENIS MEDRI* COLOURS BY *BEN WILSONHAM* LETTERS BY *MIKE STOCK*

THEY ARE YOUNG, AND THEY STUMBLE, BUT THEY HAVE MADE *GREAT STRIDES* SINCE I CAME HERE.

THEY CANNOT EVEN STOP FROM *FIGHTING THEMSELVES*, AND *HATE* THOSE THAT ARE DIFFERENT.

THEY HAVE FOUGHT FOR THE RIGHTS OF EACH OTHER, BROUGHT *DEMOCRACY* AND *FREEDOM* TO THOSE LOCKED IN *TYRANNY* AND *FEAR*.

AND AS FOR FIGHTING *THEMSELVES*, THAT MADNESS YOU HAVE BROUGHT HERE UPON OUR *OWN PEOPLE* NOW *TOO*!

THEY ARE A *DANGER* TO US!

HOLD, ALLIES AND SISTERS, *ALL!* HOLD!

THIS *FARCE* IS *OVER*!

THE *ONLY* DANGER TO *OUR PEOPLE*, SISTER, IS *YOU!*

189

A DETECTIVE CALLS

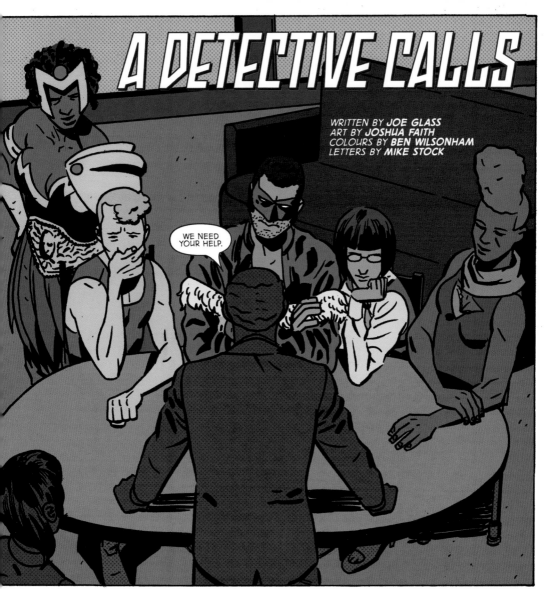

WRITTEN BY **JOE GLASS**
ART BY **JOSHUA FAITH**
COLOURS BY **BEN WILSONHAM**
LETTERS BY **MIKE STOCK**

WE NEED YOUR HELP.

THIS GUY'S GOING AROUND IN A *GIANT* SUIT OF ARMOUR AND HE'S PULLING PEOPLE APART.

IN ONE CASE, *LITERALLY*.

HE'S CALLING HIMSELF *OUTRAGE*, BUT HE'S NOT THE ORIGINAL GUY. HIM WE *LIKED*. THIS GUY...

THIS GUY'S A *KILLER*.

YEAH, FROM WHAT WE HEARD, HE'S KILLING *GAY BASHERS* AND *HOMOPHOBES*.

GOOD RIDDANCE TO *BAD TRASH*, HONEY.

ANGEL!

I HAVE A QUESTION: WHERE DID THIS GUY GET *ALL* THE TOOLS AND EQUIPMENT HE NEEDED TO MAKE THE SUIT? I MEAN, *IT LOOKS* KINDA COMPLEX.

WING IS A FORMER EMPLOYEE OF WILDE INDUSTRIES.

HE WAS A *HIGH UP* IN EXPERIMENTAL TECHNOLOGIES, *SPECIALISING* IN BODY ARMOURS AND TOOLS FOR *EXTREME SITUATIONS*.

OH.

I'M SORRY, HONEY, BUT I *STILL* DON'T SEE WHY WE SHOULD STOP HIM. HE'S NOT HURTING ANYONE WHO DON'T DESERVE IT.

AND NO WORSE THAN ANYTHING *THEY'VE* DONE T'OTHERS...

E 'N' BEAR GOT CALLED WHILE TROLLING ONCE. A GAY KID AS BEING *BEATEN UP* UNDER BRIDGE IN CENTRAL PARK.

WE RAN, *FASTER* THAN I THINK I *EVER* RUN BEFORE.

BUT WE WERE *TOO* LATE.

KID WAS *BARELY RECOGNISABLE*. THEY *WOULDN'T* EVEN LET HIS *MAMMA* SEE HIM, STATE HE WAS IN.

LISTEN, *I UNDERSTAND*, BUT THIS MONSTER *NEEDS* TO BE STOPPED.

AND IT'S *NOT* JUST THE VICTIMS OF HIS *OWN* ATTACKS HE'S HURT NOW EITHER.

THE KID HE WAS *'SAVING'* IN HIS LAST ATTACK...

KID WAS *SAT* THERE, WATCHING AS THIS *MONSTROSITY* CAME LIKE A *BAT OUTTA HELL* AND PUT THE BEAT DOWN ON A MAN LIKE *NOTHIN'* BEFORE.

SURE, THE GUY HAD BEEN *KICKI* HIM IN THE GUT ONLY *MOMENTS* BEFORE, BUT HE WAS *MORE SCA* OF THIS *HULKIN* BEAST, I IMAGIN.

HE *EVEN* HAD TO WATCH A MAN GET *RIPPED* IN TWO... HEARD THE SOUND OF HIS SKIN AND BONE *TEARIN'*...

I SAY *'IMAGINE'* 'CAUSE THE KID HASN'T MADE A SOUND SINCE THAT NIGHT. HE'S TOO *TERRIFIED* TO LEAVE HIS BED.

OUTRAGE HAS *DESTROYE* HIM JUST AS *BADLY* AS H DID THE KIDS' ATTACKER.

196

HOW *LONG* BEFORE HE STARTS KILLING WITNESSES? WHETHER BY ACCIDENT *OR* ON PURPOSE.

AND *NEXT* TIME--

STOP. WE'RE ON IT, DETECTIVE WILLIAMS.

YES, *DARLING.* LIKE THEM OR NOT, NO ONE *DESERVES* TO BE SUMMARILY *ENDED* IN SUCH A *GRISLY* MANNER.

I'M *HAPPY* TO PUNISH THOSE THAT *DESERVE IT,* BUT THERE MUST *ALWAYS* BE A LINE.

FIIIIIINE!

SO, WHAT'S THE PLAN, *BIG GUY?*

GOOD.

WE HAVE A GUY IN CUSTODY, BEAT UP *THREE* GAY KIDS WITH A *GANG OF THUGS* TWO WEEKS AGO.

IT'S *SECOND* OFFENSE. WE'RE GONNA LET HIM OFF ON A TECHNICALITY.

AH, *BAIT.* HOW DELIGHTFULLY DEVIOUS.

THANKS. WE'VE, SHALL WE SAY, *SURREPTITIOUSLY* TAGGED THE GUY. WE WANT *YOU* TO KEEP AN EYE ON HIM, WAIT FOR *OUTRAGE* TO SHOW UP. YOU IN?

WE'LL BE READY.

197

The Pride Adventures Issue 3 - Cover by Jamal Campbell

199

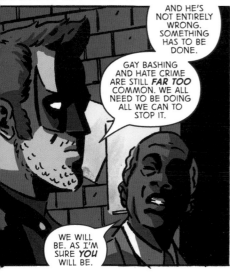

SO, IT'S DONE, THEN. KID'S GOING TO JAIL.

YEAH... BUT THE MENTAL ANGUISH HE WENT THROUGH, IT'LL BE TAKEN INTO ACCOUNT. HE'LL BE PUNISHED FOR WHAT HE'S DONE, BUT FAIRLY.

AND WHAT OF THE VILE LITTLE ROTTERS HE'D BEEN STOPPING, DARLING?

JAI GOT HIS REVENGE THE FIRST TIME HE VENTURED OUT. ALL THE OTHERS WERE JUST HIM TRYING TO STAY CLOSE TO LEWIS... IN ENTIRELY THE WRONG WAY.

BUT WHO'S–

GOING TO KEEP PEOPLE SAFE FROM THEM? THAT WOULD BE *US*, WOULDN'T IT?

SO YOU GOT THE CRAZY *FAGGOT?* GUESS IT TAKES A HOMO TO CATCH A HOMO, HUH?

210

OUTRAGE

WRITTEN BY *JOE GLASS*
LAYOUTS BY *CORY SMITH* & *JD FAITH*
ART BY *JD FAITH*
COLORS BY *BEN WILSONHAM*
LETTERS BY *MIKE STOCK*

YOU CAN'T GO HOME AGAIN

END OF THE LINE, *POKER FACE!*

WRITER
JOE GLASS
ART
MARTIN KIRBY
COLOURS
BEN WILSONHAM
LETTERS
MIKE STOCK

YOU OKAY?

SHE'S GETTING AWAY!

WE WON'T CATCH HER NOW. *TRUST ME,* SHE'LL SHOW AGAIN. SHE ALWAYS DOES.

WHAT'S HER DEAL ANYWAY? DID SHE FALL?

NOPE, JUMPED.

POKER FACE IS JUST AS HER NAME IMPLIES: UNPREDICTABLE, ALWAYS A MILLION STEPS AHEAD, AND *DAMN* LUCKY.

SOME PEOPLE THINK IT'S A POWER, BUT NO ONE'S EVER HELD ONTO HER LONG ENOUGH TO CHECK.

WHAT YOU DOIN' HERE ANYWAY, KID?

I WAS, UH, IN THE AREA.

UH HUH.

THEY CALLED AGAIN, HUH?

...

THERE REALLY IS NO KEEPING ANYTHING FROM YOU, IS THERE.

LATER

I MEAN, THEY SENT ME AWAY... TRIED TO *CURE* ME LIKE I WAS SICK. WHY WOULD THEY WANT ME BACK?

WHY WOULD *I* WANT *THEM?*

BECAUSE THEY'RE YOUR PARENTS, OWEN.

BUT I HAVEN'T CHANGED. I *WON'T.*

AND THAT DOESN'T MATTER. THEY'RE *STILL* YOUR PARENTS. YOU'RE *STILL* THEIR SON.

THAT'S SADLY MORE THAN A LOT OF PEOPLE GET. I NEVER GOT THE CHANCE TO SHARE EVERYTHING ABOUT MYSELF WITH MY PARENTS.

I'LL NEVER KNOW WHAT THEY'D HAVE THOUGHT OF THE MAN I BECAME.

AND SURE, *MAYBE* THEY HAVEN'T CHANGED EITHER, BUT IF YOU *DON'T* GO, YOU'LL ALWAYS WONDER.

AND THAT'S A BURDEN FEW CAN BARE. THEY'RE REACHING OUT TO YOU...

...MAYBE YOU SHOULD GIVE THEM A CHANCE.

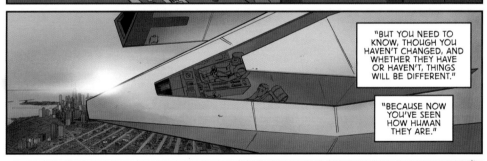

"BUT YOU NEED TO KNOW, THOUGH YOU HAVEN'T CHANGED, AND WHETHER THEY HAVE OR HAVEN'T, THINGS WILL BE DIFFERENT."

"BECAUSE NOW YOU'VE SEEN HOW HUMAN THEY ARE."

"THE WORLD IS *FULL* OF PEOPLE AFRAID OF WHAT'S DIFFERENT. AND SOMETIMES, WHEN IT COMES WITHIN THEIR HOMES, THEIR FAMILIES, THEY *LASH OUT.*"

"BUT THAT TRIAL GIVES 'EM THE OPPORTUNITY TO GROW. *TO LEARN.*"

"AND MOVE ON. BUT WE'LL ONLY MOVE ON IF WE TAKE THE RISK."

HE MORNING AFTER

RITTEN BY JOE GLASS   ART BY ADAM GRAPHITE   LETTERS BY MIKE STOCK

COME ON, I DON'T THINK WE'RE THE FIRST ONES UP FOR A CH--

OH, HI!

WHA-?!

UH, HI. I'M HARRY. I, UMM, I'M FABMAN'S... FRIEND.

UGH. MORNIN'.

YAWN

≥GULP≤

MORNING, CUB.

SORRY ABOUT THAT. HE'S A VERY... CONFIDENT GUY.

BUT HE HAD AN—

WELL, DUDE. IT IS THE MORNING...

BELIEVE IT OR NOT, HE'S STRAIGHT. BUT HE JUST DOESN'T SEEM TO MIND BEING... WELL, BARE AS THE DAY HE WAS BORN IN FRONT OF GAY DUDES.

SOMEONE SHOULD REALLY TALK TO THE KID ABOUT WEARING SOME CLOTHES IN COMPANY.

GOD-DAMMIT, CUB, PUT SOME CLOTHES ON!

RUNNING ORDER

WOLF

Written by Joe Glass, Art by Marc Ellerby

WHITE TRASH

Written by Joe Glass, Art by Joshua Faith

ANGEL

Story and Art by Joe Glass, Colors by Kris Carter, Letters by Mike Stock

MUSCLE MARY

Written by Joe Glass, Art by Cory Smith, Colors by Kris Carter, Letters by Mike Stock

BEAR

Written by Joe Glass, Art by Ryan Cody, Letters by Mike Stock

FABMAN

Written by Joe Glass, Art by Jack Lawrence, Letters by Mike Stock

FROST

Written by Joe Glass, Art by Héctor Barros, Letters by Mike Stock

TWINK

Written by Joe Glass, Art by Jacopo Camagni, Letters by Mike Stock

WOLF

"SO, LIKE, YOU GUYS THINK THIS... *WOLF* DUDE SHOULD BE IN *THE JUSTICE DIVISION?*"

WORDS: JOSEPH GLASS
ART: MARC ELLERBY

IN HIS CIVILIAN IDENTITY, WHICH IS PUBLICLY UNKNOWN, WOLF IS *BRIAN WILDE*, HEAD OF THE MASSIVE ENERGY, ENVIRONMENTAL AND PROPRIETARY TECHNOLOGY CONCERN *WILDE CORPORATION.*

INHERITED WHEN HIS PARENTS DIED IN A *CAR CRASH* WHEN HE WAS JUST *17* YEARS OF AGE, HE'D ALREADY SPENT MANY YEARS TRAINING HIS BODY AND MIND FOR WHAT HE SAW AS HIS PERSONAL MISSION.

HE HAS NO POWERS, INSTEAD WORKING HARD TO REACH PEAK PHYSICAL FITNESS. HE HAS TRAINED IN NUMEROUS MARTIAL ARTS. WITH HIS RESOURCES, HE CREATES ANY EQUIPMENT HE NEEDS.

HE'S TRAINED HIS MIND TOO, GRADUATING WITH DEGREES IN CRIMINOLOGY, CHEMISTRY AND BUSINESS.

KRAKOW!

IN HIS HOME OF CHICAGO, HE'S ACHIEVED HIS *GREATEST* SUCCESS.

Chicago Tribune

WOLF WINS

Crime fighter takes on mob and wins.

PROVING A MASTER INVESTIGATOR TOO, HE TOOK DOWN EVERY SINGLE CRIME BOSS IN ONE FELL SWOOP, PROVIDING ENOUGH EVIDENCE TO PUT THEM ALL AWAY FOR GOOD.

"COOL.

OKAY, DUDE. I GET IT. THIS GUY'S PRETTY GOOD, HUH.

'KAY, I GUESS HE'S IN.

COOL."

WOLF
a.k.a. Brian Wilde

Powers:
Peak physical fitnes
Martial arts.
Keen scientific mind
and detective.

THE BEAR

WRITTEN BY JOE GLASS
ILLUSTRATED BY RYAN CODY
LETTERED BY MIKE STOCK

I WEREN'T ALWAYS THE MAN-BEAR I AM TODAY.

WELL, I GUESS I WAS ALWAYS A 'BEAR', HUH, JUST NOT *THE* BEAR!

AN' MOREOVER, I WEREN'T ALWAYS GAY EITHER. OR I WAS, BUT I WASN'T... COMFORTABLE WITH IT.

I WAS RAISED TO BELIEVE IN FAMILY, A GOOD, HARD DAYS WORK. AND I... I MARRIED SARAH, THINKING THAT MY HEART WOULD GET INTO THAT SOMEDAY TOO.

LIKE I SAID, I WAS UNCOMFORTABLE IN MY OWN SKIN. MY HEART KNEW IT...

...MY BODY WOULD SOON TOO.

WHAT I THOUGHT WAS A BAD CASE A' FLU TURNED OUT TO BE SO MUCH MORE.

I WAS X-CEL VIRUS POSITIVE, I WAS JUST A LATE BLOOMER...IN MORE'N ONE CASE.

SARAH CERTAINLY DIDN'T TAKE TO THE NEW LOOK, CAN'T BLAME 'ER. BUT SHE REALLY HATED THE MAGAZINES...

I'M... I'M SORRY, BABY. BUT I THINK... I THINK I'M GAY.

SHE LEFT ME AFTER THAT. CAN'T BLAME 'ER. WOULDN'T HEAR FROM HER AGAIN IN YEARS, BUT THEN, I WASN'T THINKING MUCH ABOUT THAT THEN.

I FINALLY CAME TO TERMS WITH WHO I WAS, BUT IT WAS SO LATE... I HAD NO IDEA WHAT I WAS DOING.

I WASN'T REALLY THINKING AT THIS TIME. I DID THINGS. THINGS I AIN'T PROUD OF.

MANHOLE

AND I MADE MISTAKES.

MISTAKES THAT'LL AFFECT THE REST OF MY LIFE.

BUT HEY, WE ALL MAKE MISTAKES.

IT'S HOW WE LIVE WITH 'EM; WHAT WE DO AFTERWARDS THAT COUNTS.

FOR ME, I EDUCATE KIDS ON THE SCENE SO THEY DON'T MAKE THE SAME MISTAKES I DO.

AND HEY, I'M STRONG, SO I DO MY PART TO PROTECT MY COMMUNITY TOO, ANY WAY I CAN.

AND LUCKILY I FOUND GOOD FRIENDS ALONG THE WAY TO HELP ME OUT.

THE BEAR

AK.

HARVEY CASTRO

POWER:
ANIMAL KEEN SENSE.
ENHANCED STRENGT
AND AGILITY. BEAR-LIK
APPEARANCE

SO THA'S ME. I FIGHT FOR WHAT'S RIGHT, NO MATTER WHAT.

'CAUSE WE ALL MAKE MISTAKES, BU' WE DON'T HAVE TO BE DEFINED BY 'EM.

by **JOE GLASS**

JACK LAWRENCE

by **MIKE STOCK**

FABMAN

STEPHEN WAINRIGHT ALWAYS KNEW HE WAS GAY. HIS PARENTS WOULD TELL HIM THAT THEY ALWAYS DID TOO, WHEN HE CAME OUT AT THE AGE OF JUST FIFTEEN YEARS. AND THEY WOULD TELL HIM THEY WERE PROUD.

WHICH WAS GOOD, BECAUSE SO WAS HE.

ALSO ALWAYS KNEW THAT HE ANTED TO HELP PEOPLE. AND WAS ALWAYS AT HIS BEST LPING PEOPLE JUST LIKE HIM.

HETHER IT WAS ORGANISING MARCHES R GAY PRIDE EVENTS, OR COUNSELLING OSE AFFECTED BY HIV OR GAY SHING ATTACKS, STEPHEN WAS THERE R THEM ALL. STEPHEN WAS ALWAYS ERE TO OFFER A PIECE OF HOPE.

HE EVEN OPENED A CLUB SO PEOPLE COULD RELAX AND HAVE A PLACE TO HAVE A GOOD NIGHT OUT TOGETHER. SO COMMITTED WAS HE TO HIS COMMUNITY, HIS WHOLE LIFE HAD BEGUN TO REVOLVE AROUND IT.

WHICH IS WHY HE WAS PERFECT FOR US.

STEPHEN WAINRIGHT.

E WATCHED YOU OUR PLANET IN DROMEDA A FOR SOME AND WE OU Y.

WE OFFER YOU THE POWER TO HELP OTHERS LIKE YOU. TO BE A BEACON OF HOPE AND UNDERSTANDING, AND BRING PEACE TO THOSE THAT HAVE YET TO ACCEPT YOU AND YOURS.

ME? REALLY? OH MY GOD...

YES, STEPHEN. YOU WERE CHOSEN FOR YOUR SENSE OF PRIDE IN WHO YOU ARE AND THE STRENGTH YOU FIND IN THAT AND OFFER TO OTHERS. WE OFFER YOU A GREAT POWER TO SPREAD YOUR MESSAGE FURTHER.

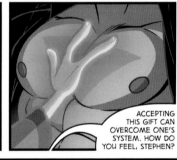

ACCEPTING THIS GIFT CAN OVERCOME ONE'S SYSTEM. HOW DO YOU FEEL, STEPHEN?

FABULOUS!

FROM THAT DAY FORTH, STEPHEN HAS CALLED HIMSELF FABMAN AND DONNED A COSTUME AS IS THE CUSTOM OF THE EARTH HEROES.

HE HAS FOUGHT TIRELESSLY TO SAVE THOSE THAT NEED SAVING, AND TO SPREAD A MESSAGE OF ACCEPTANCE AND LOVE WHEREVER HE GOES.

AND THUS, LIKE STEPHEN, LIKE HIS PARENTS, WE TOO FIND OURSELVES... PROUD.

FABMAN

A.K.A. STEPHEN WAINRIGHT

POWERS: ABLE TO GENERATE MULTICOLOURED LIGHT, EACH COLOUR HAVING DIFFERENT CAPABILITIES SUCH AS SUPER-STRENGTH, SPEED, HEAT AND FLIGHT.

FROST

THANKS FOR TAKING THE TIME, *MS...*?

FROST, DEAR.

RIGHT. SO, WE ALREADY KNOW YOU WERE BORN INTO AN ARISTOCRATIC FAMILY IN THE UK. YOU NEVER WANTED FOR ANYTHING.

WELL, EXCEPT FOR POWERS IT SEEMS. WE KNOW YOURS *AREN'T* NATURAL.

YOU HAD EXTENSIVE SURGERY TO ENHANCE CERTAIN... ATTRIBUTES, *AND* GIVE YOU YOUR ICE MANIPULATION POWERS.

WELL, YOU'VE DONE *VERY WELL* BY YOURSELF SO FAR, DEARIE.

WE JUST NEED *YOU* TO FILL IN THE GAPS.

MY EDITOR WANTS A COMPREHENSIVE STORY.

LIKE, WE KNOW THAT AFTER YOUR SURGERIES, YOUR FAMILY DISOWNED YOU.

BUT WE *DON'T* KNOW WHY.

YOU'RE FAMILY NAME WAS RYDER, *RIGHT?* YOU HAD A BROTHER BY THE NAME OF... *EDWARD?*

VERY *GOOD.* VERY GOOD *INDEED.*

TELL ME, YOU'RE STORY. IT'S *ALL* ON THERE?

UMM, YEAH, I...

HEY! WHAT THE HELL?!

I PAID *A LOT* OF MONEY TO MAKE MYSELF WHAT I AM TODAY.

THE *ICE-COLD* HEADMISTRESS KEEPING THE MASSES IN LINE.

I PAID *EVEN MORE* TO MAKE MY PAST *DISAPPEAR.*

IT WOULDN'T COST MUCH MORE TO MAKE SURE IT *STAYS* THAT WAY.

REMEMBE THAT, WON'T Y DARLING?

WRITTEN BY JOE GLASS

ART BY HECTOR BARROS

LETTERS BY MIKE STOCK

A.K.A. EVANGELINE ISOBELLA RYDER I POWERS: ICE AND TEMPERATURE MANIPU

TWINK

WRITTEN BY *JOE GLASS*
ART BY *JACOPO CAMAGNI*
LETTERS BY *MIKE STOCK*

DEAR MOM AND DAD,

I SUPPOSE YOU SHOULD KNOW THAT I'M OKAY...IF YOU REALLY CARE. I'M WRITING THIS LETTER TO TRY AND FIGURE THAT OUT MYSELF.

IT'S NOT LIKE IT WAS A SURPRISE I WANTED TO BE A SUPERHERO. IT'S ALL I EVER WANTED TO BE.

I ACTUALLY TRAINED FOR IT THOUGH. I WAS GOING TO BE THE BEST. WHETHER I HAD POWERS OR NOT.

I WON AT SPORTS, I WORKED HARD. BUT ALL YOU GUYS EVER SAW WAS HOW 'DANGEROUSLY' DIFFERENT I WAS BECOMING.

THEN ONE DAY...

GET OUTTA TH' WAY!

OH MY GOD!

...THE X-CEL VIRUS FINALLY REACTED WITH MY GENES AND I FINALLY GOT ALL I WANTED.

I'D NEVER BEEN HAPPIER.

YEEE EEAA AAAH!

BUT NOT YOU GUYS.

INSTEAD, YOU SEND ME TO A PRISON CAMP, RUN BY A MAD MAN WHO CLAIMED HE COULD 'CURE' ME.

AND YOU LEFT ME.

WELL, I GOT OUT OF THAT PLACE. I WON'T TELL YOU WHERE I AM.

AND I'M GONNA FIND PEOPLE JUST LIKE ME AND BE HAPPY AGAIN.

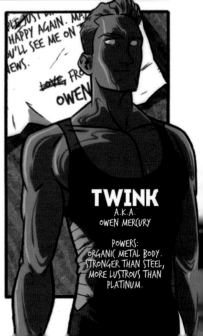

...JUST BE HAPPY AGAIN. MAY YOU'LL SEE ME ON T NEWS.

~~LOVE~~ FRO OWEN

TWINK
A.K.A.
OWEN MERCURY

POWERS:
ORGANIC METAL BODY. STRONGER THAN STEEL, MORE LUSTROUS THAN PLATINUM.

BONUS MATERIAL

R U N N I N G
O R D E R

OH, NO SHE BETTER DON'T

Written by Joe Glass, Art by Gavin Mitchell, Letters by Mike Stock

GUN MACHINE

Written by Joe Glass, Art by Andy W Clift, Colors by Ben Wilsonham, Letters by Mike Stock

OPEN UP

Written by Joe Glass, Art by Tana Ford, Colors by Ben Wilsonham, Letters by Mike Stock

MILKSHAKE

Written by Mike Garley, Art by Chris Imber, Colors by Ben Wilsonham, Letters by Mike Stock

COME TOGETHER

Written by Joe Glass, Art by Andy Bennett, Letters by Mike Stock

THE PACK

Written by Joe Glass, Art by Ben Wilsonham, Letters by Mike Stock

CARDIFF MARDI GRAS, THE CITY'S ANNUAL LGBTQ EVENT.

GOOD EVENING, CARDIFF! AND WELCOME TO *MY* NIGHT!

DRAG EXT??VAGANZA!!

AFTER ALL, YA CAN'T HAVE A DRAG EXTRAVAGANZA WITHOUT THE GREATEST DRAG QUEEN IN THE WORLD, IMA SUPERSTAR!

YOU SUCK!

OH, AND DID I FORGET TO MENTION, HONEY?

I ALSO HAVE SUPERPOWERS!

'CAUSE I'M THE MOST FIERCE, *SUPERPOWERED* DRAG QUEEN IN THE WORLD!

UH UH, HONEY...

236

OH, NO SHE BETTER DON'T

YOU AIN'T SNATCHING *THAT* TITLE!

written by **JOE GLASS**   art by **GAVIN MITCHELL**   letters by **MIKE STOCK**

ANGEL! AND YOUR NEW TEAM...

...HEARD YOU WEREN'T FIERCE ENOUGH TO HEAD OUT ALONE ANYMORE.

BUT YOU MUST BE DELUDED IF YA THINK YOU CAN BEAT *IMA SUPERSTAR!*

DON'T YOU JUST *LOVE* IT WHEN THEY START USING THE THIRD PERSON.

UH HUH, HONEY.

GUYS, LET'S STOP THIS FOOL.

C'MON, GUYS... LET'S DO THIS!

TRYING TO SCARE ME BY BEING ALL *BIG BAD?*

OH, HONEY...

237

you can follow the adventures of angel and co. in

THE PRIDE

TIMES SQUARE, NEW YORK

YA WANT TO TAKE OUR GUNS! IT'S OUR *CONSTITUTIONAL RIGHT!* YOU WON'T TAKE *MY RIGHTS* FROM ME!

OY... REALLY?

READY, TWINK?

OH, YOU HAVE *NO* IDEA... BOMBS AWAY, FABS!

TNK

GUN MACHINE

WRITTEN BY JOE GLASS - ART BY ANDY CLIFT
COLORS BY BEN WILSONHAM - LETTERS BY MIKE STOCK

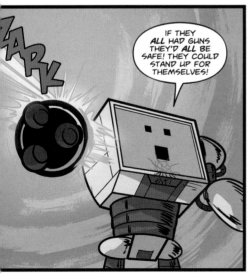

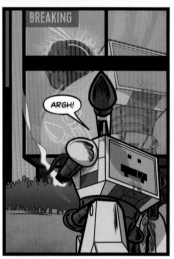

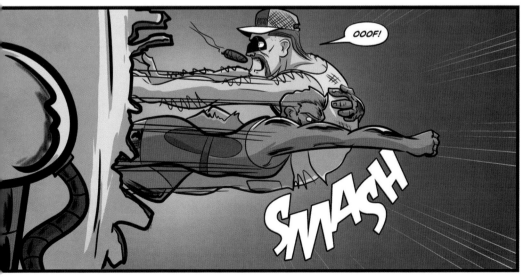

OPEN UP

TTEN BY
E GLASS

BY
A FORD

ORS BY
N WILSONHAM

ERS BY
E STOCK

I HAD NO IDEA YOUR AXE COULD DO THAT, DARLING.

THE GIFT OF ATHENA IS NO MERE AXE.

IT IS A TOOL GIFTED TO THE SAPPHONS BY THE GODDESSES, ABLE TO TAKE SHAPE AS WHATEVER IT IS WE NEED.

THE LABRYS IS MAYBE ITS TRUE SHAPE, BUT IT IS SO MUCH MORE.

WELL, I'M GLAD... COULDN'T HAVE MY NEW GIRLFRIEND FILLED WITH NEW HOLES.

HA! WE ARE 'GIRLFRIENDS' NOW THEN?

MUSCLE MARY... SAPPHIRE? CAN WE GO SOMEWHERE A BIT MORE... PRIVATE?

YOUR WISH IS MY COMMAND.

YOU KNOW HOW HARD IT IS FOR ME TO BE SO... OPEN WITH PEOPLE. BUT SAPPHIRE, IF WE ARE GOING TO BE TOGETHER, THEN I NEED YOU TO KNOW THE TRUTH.

I DON'T SHOUT ABOUT IT BECAUSE IT IS NO ONE ELSE'S BUSINESS, BUT YOU... YOU I NEED TO BE COMPLETELY HONEST WITH.

YOU KNOW I FEEL THE SAME, BUT HONESTLY, EVANGELINA, THERE IS NOTHING YOU COULD TELL ME THAT WOULD CHANGE HOW I FEEL.

SAPPHIRE. I'M TRANS.

I... I WASN'T ALWAYS... I DIDN'T ALWAYS LOOK LIKE THIS.

I--

'LINA, SHHH.

I DON'T CARE.

WRITTEN BY MIKE GARLEY – ART BY CHRIS IMBER
COLORS BY BEN WILSONHAM – LETTERS BY MIKE STOCK

249

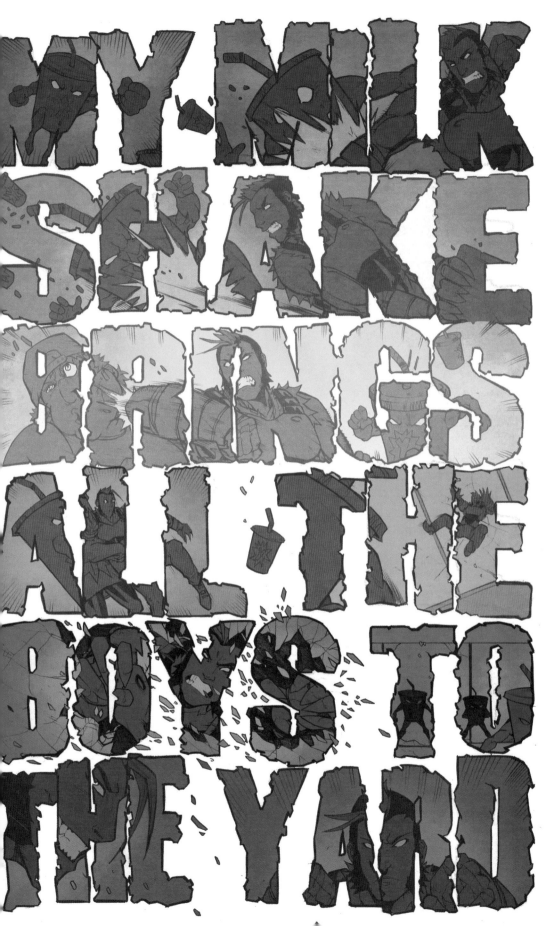

THE END.

COME TOGETHER

written by
JOE GLASS
art by
ANDY BENNETT
letters by
MIKE STOCK

THIS STORY TAKES PLACE DURING EVENTS OF THE PRIDE #1.

THANKS EVERYONE FOR COMING OUT TO SUPPORT THE CASTRO FUND, HELPING THOSE LIVING WITH H.I.V. AND AIDS.

NOW, I DON'T CARE WHERE YOU GO, BUT YA CAN'T STAY HERE, SO GET ON OUT!

THANKS, EVERYONE, REALLY!

OKAY, HONEY. I'M GONNA GO ON PATROL AND MAKE SURE THESE BABIES DON'T GET NO TROUBLE OUT THERE.

I'LL BE RIGHT BEHIND YOU.

AND THANKS, ANGEL. TONIGHT MEANS A LOT.

ANY TIME, HONEY. I'LL HEAD OUT THE BACK.

DAMN... I LOVE IT WHEN THE COMMUNITY COMES TOGETHER LIKE THIS...

WHAT THE HELL!

DON'T TOUCH ME!

DIRTY, DISEASE-SPREADING W*@R&!

253

JUST... IS IT ENOUGH? AM I MAKING A DIFFERENCE AT ALL?

WHY CAN'T OUR COMMUNITY COME TOGETHER AND FIGHT FOR WHAT'S RIGHT?

WHY... WHY DO I EVEN BOTHER?

HIYA, BEAR! YOU THINK YOU MIGHT BE INTERESTED IN WORKING TOGETHER ON SOMETHING?

I THINK IT MIGHT BE JUST THE THING YOU'RE LOOKING FOR.

BECAUSE IT'S THE RIGHT THING TO DO.

HUH?

UH, SURE, FABMAN...

FABULOUS! COME ROUND FANTABULOSA TOMORROW NIGHT! OH, AND BRING ANGEL TOO!

ANGEL! I COMPLETELY FORGOT! I BETTER GO FIND HER!

WE'LL BE THERE, FABS.

THANK YOU!

JUST THE BEGINNING...

THE PACK
A PRIDE STORY

WRITTEN BY
JOE GLASS

ART BY
BEN WILSONHAM

LETTERS BY
MIKE STOCK

THE RED TIGERS HAVE BEEN MAKING MEETINGS LIKE THIS ALL OVER CHICAGO.

THIS IS THE FIRST TIME I'VE BEEN HERE IN TIME TO CATCH THE DEALER.

ME AGAINST THESE FIVE...

...THIS SHOULD BE *FUN*.

TAKING OUT THE ARMED IDIOTS FIRST SHOULD BE EASY.

FAST AND HARD. JUST TAKE 'EM DOWN.

DAMN! SHOOT 'IM ALREADY!

YOU THINK I AIN'T TRYIN'?!

A COUPLE TASER-DISCS TAKE DOWN THE OTHER TWO.

DEALER IS NEXT.

THE KEY IS TO FIGHT SMART.

SMALL, CRITICAL STRIKES.

TAKING DOWN THE TARGET WITH A THOUSAND CUTS.

TAKE OUT THE HAMSTRING. IMMOBILISE THE TARGET.

OR NOT.

TECHNOLOGICAL AUGMENTATION IS FAIRLY COMMON.

IN A WORLD WHERE PEOPLE GET SUPERPOWERS, THOSE THAT DON'T OFTEN TRY TO FIND WAYS TO LEVEL THE PLAYING FIELD.

NOT EVERYONE CAN AFFORD THE KINDS OF BIOLOGICAL AND GENETIC AUGMENTATION THAT FROST HAS.

NOT SEEN THIS LEVEL OF AUGMENTATION IN... EVER.

BEHIND THE SCENES

GAVIN MITCHELL

was a fairly difficult
acter to come up with
sign for, and I really just
a vague idea on the kind
ro that Wolf was, and
e random ideas for look.
vound up with a ton of
ns, but finally settled
e fantastic design from
n that people have really
onded to.

GAVIN MITCHELL

My one suggestion for Gav on WT was to look at the model/artist/actor Trevor Wayne... which of course meant lots of tattoos. I'm sure all the artists on the series loved me for that.

Originally, Frost was a blonde and wore all white, but we felt that this made her look too similar to a character belonging to a certain House of Ideas.

We had a few design ideas to redesign the character, and sort of ultimately went with a kind of Marlene Dietrich vibe.

Kris redesigned Outrage for his second appearance onward, to suggest Jai Wing continuing to upgrade his tech. As you can see, he included a reference for where the wearer is in the suit. It was Kris who came up with the floating gauntlets/hands idea, and I admit, initially I was reticent. But then the action sequence possibilities started flooding into my mind, and it just cemented my assertion that Kris is a creative genius!

Kris started working on these awesome bust sketches for the whole team (below), which are just incredible.

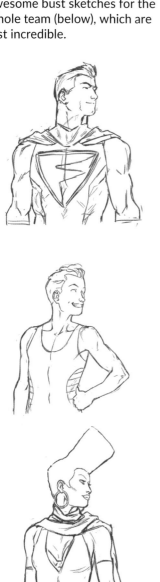

...s design for the King Lion
...n who appeared in The
... Adventures #2 (right).

...e unused cover design
...s (below).

SOPHIE CAMPBELL

Sophie found the time to h
design the last member of
Pride, who was joining in a
issue, and came up with th
final design for Bear's son,

W SCOTT FORBES

es came on to do the cover
he Pride Adventures #2,
also helped to design villain
r Face who would appear
e next issue.

reated this fantastic design
inspiration sheet for the
acter.

pomberstyle
jacket

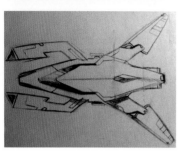

Maxime's designs for The Pride's jet, the Cruiser (left).

Maxime had to create detailed character notes and design sheets, that really added new levels of detail and distinction to the characters.

MAXIME GARBARINI

HECTOR BARROS

Maxime, with fellow artist Hector Barros, had also started working on these individual character shots to get a feel for the team. They finished Frost, FabMan and Angel, and here's also the linew for a Bear piece.

JOE GLASS

a few of the characters,
de some sketches myself.
can probably see why
't tend to draw very often.

MARTIN KIRBY

Martin came on to actually
draw the story containing
Poker Face, and expanded and
streamlined the original design
for the character.

Here's some variations on his
final design.

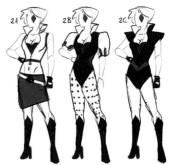

THE PRIDE
BEAR

THE PRIDE
CUB

THE PRIDE ADVENTURES · THE LIONESSES

Chris did some much neede
character design sheets to
feel for some of the charac
appearing in his pages (this
page and overleaf).

Chris did the design for the
Lionesses, the back-up/
lieutenants in King Lion's ga
(bottom left).

Because Christian is an
incredible talent, he just ha
create a working plan for th
training room too (overleaf)

HRISTIAN WILDGOOSE

THE PRIDE
TWINK

THE PRIDE
WOLF

THE PRIDE
TRAINING ROOM

TRAINING DROID

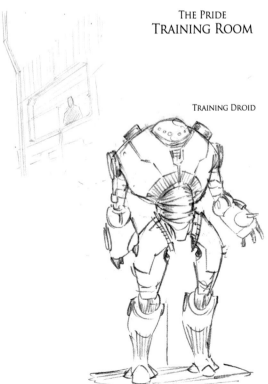

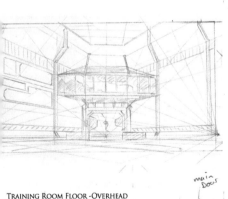

TRAINING ROOM FLOOR - OVERHEAD

main door

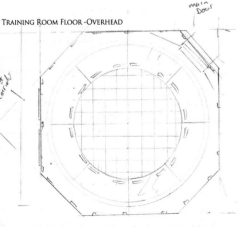

AFTERWORD

Well, that's it, everyone.

All of *The Pride*, and more, in one place. And we couldn't have done it without you.

I want to say a massive thank you again to everyone who has funded through the Kickstarter, but also to all those who have been supporting *The Pride* from day one.

The book has been coming out now for seven years. A lengthy, and at times difficult and frustrating production, every bit of which has been a lesson and welcome challenge. The support from all of the readers, and those who have come and talked to me at cons about the themes and story of the project, has made every second of the journey absolutely worthwhile. That my little idea can be something that others enjoy and want to see in the world... there's no more gratifying and wonderful feeling than I have ever come across.

Because really *The Pride* has been going on even older. I was tinkering away with characters and scenes from way back when; those seemingly ancient days when I was a comic reading teenager coming to terms with his sexuality. All I ever wanted to see was a character that was just like me, not an allegory, not a whispered fact never appearing in the actual stories, but an open, honest and true representation. After years of uncertainty and tinkering, finally I put the idea out into the world, even if it was only for me.

Thankfully, I guess there are others out there who wanted the same thing.

Comics, as a medium, have come along a long way since we begun. Diversity and representation improves and declines in a semi-regular peak and trough, but the peaks seem to be getting higher, the troughs shallower, and when we do hit low points, the public outcry seems to be louder than ever. There's still a long way to go.

The Pride, therefore, will keep on going. I hope you decide to stay on the ride.

Joe Glass

Devin Whitlock   AlyCat   Steve McCulley   Kyla Alvey   h4wkguy
Dwayne Farver   Su Penn   Billy Potts   Asa Wilson   Jay S.
Michael Pegg   Full name is fine   Katrina L. Halliwell   Crowfeatherwolf   Slazo
Levi Fleming   Rob Tatnell   Alexandre Gallant   Alex Coonce   Ron Phillips I
HungryTigerNYC   James Blundell   A. M. Marquette   Robert Freeman   Andrew Whela
Melme   Morgan A. McLaughlin   Bill Sorensen   Teko   mk
Jacqueline Washington   McFarland   Devon T.   Carla H.   Andrew Doucet &
Ed Brenton   Shana ShadowWing   Nicole Imry   Austen Marie   Bond
Sarah Zaidan   Leon & Theo   Jorge Bogarín   Andrew Nawrocki   Sammy Khan
Tricia Copeland   Daniel Kauwe   Quinn   L. Arias   Peldari
Paul Giffney   Angela Cainen   Erik Mulder   Rhiannon Raphael   Faye
Gordhan Rajani   Max Hutchison-Cockburn   James Lucas   Tibs   Sydney Stadd
Colin Oaten   Kim Colfer   Chris Welsh   Sarah Cobine   Jamilet Manza
Wally Hastings   Mike Machnikowski   Reza T   Adam C.   Caitlin Jane Hug
Jeffrey Fishman   Jake Reilly   James Boldock   Anne   Erin Subramani
Jennifer Coffin   Cavan Scott   Jeff F   Bobby Dorrance   Amy Patto
christopher cooper   Andrew Scaife   Zoe Lewycky   Dominic Quach   Chris Wilson
A. McNelis   Louise Pope   Deevon   A.J. Howard   Scully Bickha
Dan Pittman   Benedict Murray   Brookie Judge   Matt Holland   Nathan Mors
Rachel Kaplan   Sam Read   Eleanor Smith   Kian Bergstrom   Kevin C
Paul Robinson   Diane Blue   Jack Rezal   Nicholas Zakhar   Luke Ruddick
Victoria Haddow   Elisa Ady   Chace Thibodeaux   Katie Roe   Pandoraylam
Philippe Poirier   Addy the Hobbit   ElrycBathory   Alan Gerding   Nich Angell
Dexter Wong   G-Man (Comics   Foosa   Carrie Fuce   Fran Haswell-W
P. H. S.   Anonymous)   Michael Helmbrecht   Julius S. Hepp   Sean Kuprevic
Joel F. W. Price   Eric Filemyr   Rhel ná DecVandé   Amandine Texier   Karen George
Jesse Morgan   Ty Bachus   Kathleen Reed   Marius Lyseggen Krinnan   Susan Callowa
Winifred Zachery   Aurora Garvin   Michelle Rae   Secret Baroness   Rebecca Horn
Stephen Waddington   Jamie and Jonathan   Helen Collins   Benjamin Squibb   Christine Terry B
Cat Parra   Gilmour   Paul Savage   Ginny Lurcock   Aidan Kahane
Hannah Kennedy   Glen McFerren, M.D.   Jeffery Parkin   NiallG   Kristi McDowe
Hugh Griffiths   James McCulloch   Skybur   Allyson Gulihur   Comichaus.co
Camilla Markvardsen   Matt Smith   Bob Pratt   Cindy Womack   Stacy I. Barne
Malcolm Ross   Celeste D. Maisel   Pyros   Carmen Marin   Tristan Soko
Ellen Kuehnle   Pam Steele   Dennis Quertermous   Michail Dim.   Savannah Casti
Jonah Rhys McCarty   Abigail M. Walton   Addie Buenavista   Drakomathioulakis   Mel T.
Charles Grey   Matt Gosper   Nico Sprezzatura   Ginny Milway   Jonathan Bros
Jay Barnham   cloverfield   Anja Komatar   Emma Levine   Meggy Banks
Gareth Mark Williams   Tamzin Walker   Rick Hooper   Alejandra V.   Michael Barre
Kristen Madrid   Louis B.   Roger Hart   W. Scott Meeks   Sydney
James Sullhend   Rebecca Beard   Stephen Hutchison   Thomas Frank   Patrick Willem
Susie Bewell   Eric G   Matt Sanders   Zach Hauptman   Andrew Sebastian
Keiji Miashin   Victor Smith   Victoria Stolfa   Paris Marx   Sarah Kaplan
Peter Morgan   Johanna   Allan Duquette   Hyeondo Park   Ben Gerber
Rev. Ian W. Riddell   Sham Suri   Victoria E.S. Pullen   Cara   Madolyn Car
Kim Dyer   Alexandre Buron   Please leave it out   Anna Bleecker   Stephanie Gibs
Nietchaiev74   Pete Sailer   Eric K. Helgeson   Chris Dangerfield   Matt Bernsor
Tori Muller   Anima   Daphne Deadwood   Halex Pereira   Yvonne Yeh
Phil Brailey   Ryan Linn   Jenny Lutton   Jaytee Starr   Austin Wrigh
Rain & Aidenn   Gregory Lincoln   Pump-ink   Malcolm SW Wilson   Inkdrocket
Peter Blenkharn   Nicole Alfaro   Jon Gonzalez   Orlando Bennett   Jonathan 'Chadd
Drew Mayen   Jen Hickman   Nick Tyler   Tyler Mann   Chadwick
Ashkan Abousaeedi   Guilherme Prieto   Kat Pillman   Jordan Thomas   Cornell Marti
Alex MacLeod   S. Ramaj   K Van Dam   Taylor Barkley   Nadia
Frank Loose   Daniel Stalter   Tove En   Victoria C.   MayAna Creativ
Kelley Vanda   Natalia M.   Anna Owenson   Rafael Torres   Björn Bob Söder
  Amanda Lea Green   Itai Berman   Travis Lee Dill
  Jamie Lee   Calvin Hickman   Riley
  Cheryl Wong   Manuel Cervus   Dragonhide Stud
  Emily W.   Kimberly Gygi
  Ruston Ropac
  Joshua Sherwell
  Pól Stafford
  Sarah Glerup